THE BREAK OF SILENCE

"HEALING OF A BROKEN HEART"

IMANI C. SUBLETT

THE BREAK OF SILENCE; HEALING A BROKEN HEART

ISBN: 9781080291571

DEDICATION

The Break of Silence; Healing A Broken Heart, is a sequel to "A Lonely Dove." dedicated to the Outcast of America, wounded, and the broken- hearted. People, such as myself, continues to suffer from the toils of an earlier trauma in life.

We have longed for love and sacrificed more than we have ever been sacrificed for only to be stoned. There comes a time in our life that we become accustom to the rejection. No one wanted us until we had something that we could offer them. We are truly of the Bastard Nation.

After many years of rejection and let down, well, we become use to being used and being alone. By the time they begin to accept us in their lives, we do not know how to accept it and are we really accepted? How do we trust those that have used us up and then tossed us out like regurgitated bones chewed up by German shepherds?

How do we rise from the falls of those we love? How do we accept those that turned their backs on us for so many years; how do we allow ourselves to overcome the shadows of rejection? Allow yourselves to take a trip with Ava. Ava will take you on her journey of solitude and allow you inside her world of isolation and seclusion. Being able to find yourself and contentment will allow you peace and harmony.

If no one else love you; know that I love you!

ACKNOWLEDGMENTS

Giving all praises to my Lord and Savior Jesus Christ, for if it had not been for Him, I don't know where I would be. Next, I would like to thank My Lord and Savior for blessing me with my children and grandchildren. I thank Him for those that he placed in my life along the way, for the love.

The love that I have for them gave me a reason to keep fighting. Lastly, "Blood Does Not Make You Family!" Knowing that, I want to Thank and Praise God for the loved ones that I hold dearly to my heart that Christ placed in my life along the way to replace those that rejected me.

I would like to especially dedicate this novel to my Sister; The Late Tammy Yvette Casey-Frazier and Morie Lee Frazier. The bond that the three of us shared was unbreakable. While this relationship was not perfect it defined Love.

No one understood our relationship; however the extent a person would go to find love and hold on to it, clearly was defined in our relationship. Morie and I are still friends to this day and he will always be a part of my family that I hold dearly to my heart. My Christ Bless and keep him.

CHAPTER ONE

Like a child on a scorching hot summer day, I urn just to be loved like others. Hi, my name is Ava and I just want to fit in like others around me. I just want to have true friends and a real family to hangout with and spend time on vacations and have gatherings like other human beings. Was that too much to ask for?

What was so different about me? I found myself, isolated and secluded from others as a child and it continued as an adult. So many years have now passed me by; I've tried to give socialization a try, only to be shut down, abused, scorned, lied on, and used like a worn out carpet thrown to the curve awaiting the trash pick up.

As a child and a teenager, I learned to embrace this fate; as pen and paper; I found a corner of darkness to be my best friend. Dark rooms spoke loudly as the silence embraced me tightly. No love, no life, as the only sense of love was stripped from me. As I became the pawn on a chess board of a high bid tournament.

Like the clouds that feels the sky speaking to the scorching fields giving them a break, this was my peace and serenity in the den filled with wolves waiting to devour my soul, body, and mind; my sanity was on the line, I had to grab the waves as the sea grabs each ripple that fills the ocean.

I couldn't allow myself to drown in the soils of feces that surrounds me. A little fragile caramel skinned lost child with no one to understand the empty soul that rest within, the corner of the room, with dark curtains and dimmed lights; often the embrace of a television light, is my long-time best friend.

I was ripped and torn like shredded paper, I was torn from the bare essence, the life given from the womb. Like a criminal on trial, I had to represent myself in this freezing cold temperatures that could leave me frozen and unmovable. My life have never been a cake walk, and sacrifice was my ultimate purpose here; so I felt.

Like an endangered Maui's dolphin; the fight for this life was imperative, yet, how could I survive as a lonely calf, as I'm stripped from my mothers arms and her love, just to endure the brink of hatred that threaten my mere existence. How can I escape this disease of hatred and vials of darkness that will destroy me?

Surrounded by the twilight of iniquity, there was only one ray of sun throughout the darkness of this forced cave that I was confined too. She was amazing; although she was not perfect, she was the closet to love that I would ever get to as a child. I must grab tightly to this ray of sun and hold firmly. What did Ava mean?

You see, every since Ava could remember, she would see things that would sicken a person with a heart to it's very core. The darkness that initiated the beginning of her silence, that drove her to rest in a corner like a plant stand beautifying a running fern. The first strike against Ava was her Caramel skin complexion.

I was the wrong color for this cave or place called home that I had been bound too. I wasn't the suntanned white that was longed for by the beast in control. My hair, a sandy brown with waves and curls of natural descent. Hated by the beast, which felt as though I should have a head of cold jet black length hair.

I remember that black wide-toothed comb it kiss the side of my cheek, she pulled through my tender head of gold. Why did the beast hate me so; I couldn't call her mom, or tell you why; or could I? Breaking the Silence that spoke so loudly, like empty letters; was a major reason. withdrawn from everyone, caged in pain; wrapped in darkness.

The unbearable pain that I first remember, it begin the breaking silence to my heart at such a tender ripe age. Many people failed to understand that the growth of an unborn child growing inside a mother for thirty-six weeks at the time, is a bond that begins from conception. A feeling that a thief, burglar, or murder cannot steal from you,

When you have a loving mother, and she truly love her children and that bond is stripped by tragedy, it is a difficult task for the child as well as for the mother to overcome. A great tragedy, a lost, as if the wind was stripped from the sky and boomeranged from embracing the trees. Ava, would you please explain what you mean.

Silent becomes your best friend as you embrace your tragic loss. You see, the moment I lost my biological mother was the day I lost myself. I was tortured, only because I didn't know how to hate her. That was the day silence embraced me. People never realized that my bond begin with my mother the day of conception.

The mere essence of the fragrance that lingered off her beautiful self, the smells of her hair shampoo, and laundry detergent. Her body temperature, smiles, her unwavering love, and her pizzazz as she walked with strength and her touch left a memory that torture could not ever remove. Her beauty and that hug, would register like a voter on election.

Remember feeling your baby kick and see him or her turn? My mom was the only woman that had the pleasure of hearing my heartbeat, feeling me grow inside her and turn flips as I kicked; as she nurtured me for nine months. What many will never understand, because, they have no clue of love, it was my mother's love that kept me going.

So, why do you think that as a child or a mother, when your child is stolen, removed, or die that it wouldn't have a long-term tragic effect on both, the mother and the child? That love that my mom was filled with as she carried me, was able to fill my growing heart. the evil heart, torture, and hatred, end results is me. A potential suicidal, silent, and dark mess.

I can remember each one of my pregnancies as if it was yesterday and my oldest child is thirty-two years old. I loved each and every feeling, thought, and memory of those months where I carried them and the feeling I felt when the doctor sat there and said push and their heads crowned. Child after child, I returned over again, just to feel that feeling.

If you haven't had children, or if you were consumed with bitterness and evil, then you couldn't relate to the feelings that I am talking about. However, if you are a parent, a mother and you love your babies like I do, then you can feel the pain that embraced me as I watched my mom filled with tears, walk out the door.

I don't remember how old I was; however, I can remember a man in the driver side of the yellowish or tan looking car. I can remember someone grabbing me as I screamed and they threw me in the back of this car. There was one man driving and one man holding onto me. They were hurting me, my arm, it hurt; as I kicked and I screamed.

The next thing that I remember, I awaken in a nightmare. You see, this is the first time that I am able to "Break the Silence!" I never knew why it would take so long; however, I understand that over the year's, I had to adopt a coping mechanism in order to survive what was ahead of me as well as not having my mom.

I believe that my mom had to find a way to handle the pain of losing another child. This was a loss that wasn't asked for. Sometimes my mom was faced with decisions that was hard, yet necessary, but it was her decision to make. This time it was not in her control. It was no mistake that my mom gave birth to fourteen children.

And it was no mistake that she kept those that she could afford to keep and ensured the safety of those she couldn't. However, The decision of where and who would raise me was made by others. Although my mom chose to keep me, the decision to remove me was made by others and it wasn't Child Protective Services.

As a mom that had to bury a child before, it is not easy to handle such a loss. I believe that this is the way my mother felt as she carried all fourteen of her children. Although along the way she had to place a couple in different locations, she made that choice; Who gave anyone the right to take me place me in harms way, and rob me of my childhood.

When a child is removed from a loving mother, it's like death kissing her, like no other. Although we are forced to move on with our lives, the memories are like; standing by a casket saying goodbye; for the last time to a child that grew inside of that mom. There is a differences between a woman name on a birth certificate and a real mom.

CHAPTER TWO

In the mid to late 70s the system didn't really care about the welfare of the child or children in the state of Arkansas; pretty much like today. And if you were a child of color, you really didn't stand a chance. If an adult had the money or the connections they could and would make things happen regardless of what color you were.

Thanks to a local well-known preacher that was part of the NAACP and the Pastor of the First Baptist Church on Kitchen and Logan Street. He made the possible arrangements and connections for Ava to become a ward of Washington Street for the next few years of her life. Ava life would change forever. However, Ava life did not change for the better.

She became a permanent resident of Arkansas and the cave or what some called a home at least until she turned eighteen; so many would think. The state of Arkansas not only allowed Ava to be kidnapped they upheld this facade; they raped Ava of her identity, allowed her to be beaten like a runaway slave by her Master, and deprived her childhood.

This would be the first life altering change that sent Ava into a long life of mental illness until she learned how to cope with her tragedy including, isolation, depression, starting from a little child. Ava spent many years suffering from what we now would call Separation Anxiety Disorder and PTSD ignited by her early childhood trauma.

The kidnapping and removal of Ava from her mother was not unusual for certain families. Ava had a biological sister that this family adored and they didn't want to give her up. So, upon Ava kidnapping; although they really didn't want Ava, it became a package deal. For many years to come Ava Suffered. I was not a jealous type; I just wanted to be loved.

I always wondered why I didn't fit in or why I wasn't like all the rest. I had dreams and goals in life. I never wanted to be poor or depending on anyone, Why should my skin color depict my happiness? Why, couldn't I be happy like other people? Despite the odds against me; I worked for happiness and love regardless of how I was treated.

As a child, I did whatever I had to do to be loved. It wasn't enough. Sometimes, I wished that I could bleach my skin in order to blend in; light skinned children and teenagers were fancied by the beast, the woman that expected me to call her mama. My silence begins. I knew I was in a new world, a new environment very different from what I was accustom.

I wasn't going to escape, so now, I had to find a way to cope with the life that my grandmother had chose for me, Depression set in at an early age. I would often cry to myself as I watched the beast move from room to room. My heart was broken and my mind was in turmoil. You see, somethings I couldn't change. I didn't have the ability to change.

I couldn't change the structure of my body, the quality and thickness of my hair, and I couldn't make myself get my mom out of my head. *The Break of Silence, spoke* lightly, yet loudly in the break of darkness. The darkness in my soul from the breath stolen from my childhood; I excelled as I gasp to grab reality and a breath of air,

The beast begin to attack Ava as she begin to express her emptiness without her mother in her life, The demon within the beast was cruel and heartless. The Break of Silence would hinder Ava from reaching her fullest potential, stunt her mental and psychological growth, and send a fragile and loving tender caramel skinned toned child into despair.

As the beast begin to teach me, My ABC's and how to read; she slapped my tender skin with a full blow. My cheek redden and burning. She tells me how stupid, ignorant and retarded I was; this was her words. Tears kissed my face, embracing my cheeks. I longed for my mother: She loved me, she wanted me, and she would have never degraded me.

This begin my second flight to darkness. The beast was just the opposite of mom. She turned everyone against me, made everyone think that I was a plague, a disease, a mere maggot that needs bleaching out and sanitized from society. As the beast, she was the most psychotic, evil, demonic being that I had ever seen in my life.

A few days later, she would become gentle at times, usually when the beast attacked, she would turn around, provide you with money, and send you to the store to buy her cigarettes and then tell you that you could purchase whatever you wanted from the neighborhood store. She couldn't stand the silence, and silence is all I knew in order to survive.

My silence grew as I recognized the strange behavior from the beast. I had never in my life seen anyone of this magnitude. I was a child, a mere weakling, the fragile limb that hangs on to a strong bark as the wind rises and move the strong branches. My roots were weaken as the wind intensifies, I felt over watered, drenched, like a tornado.

As I grew older, darkness was my only peace, and silence was my only friend. I urn for greater darkness as one day the pain grew greater than Liberty herself, I seek for more darkness; and then the right moment came as I decided that capsules were my best friend and would give me the darkness and freedom from abuse.

You see, the beast had a way of playing the victim around those that would show her empathy. She knew just the right words to say to the silhouette of shadows that stood on the outside. They didn't understand the cruelness neither could they see, because they were not allowed to taste the dirt on the floor from the inside.

You're still confused; I understand, but do you? No one else have ever understood, except, Yeshua and the man in the white coat that sat behind the desk in an office with the comfortable lounging chair; He allowed you to relax for an hour. I was comfortable with him, he seem to care, no one else cared to face reality or the truth.

Being chased around the house with knives by the beast was not uncommon in this place call home. We were ordered to stay out of the beast way, as excuses were made for her behavior. She was so sick that she would falsely accuse me of trying to sleep with her husband; I was very sick one day, she came home from work and I was asleep, she beat me,

She called me all sorts of names as she beat me. Sex was the furthest thing from my mind; I was only a ripe tender age of maybe nine or so, I thought he was my daddy; he never did anything inappropriate to me. He was not that type of man. Never again would I rest on her pillow as I try to waver through the sickness that embraced my body.

The place I was forced to call home; it seemed like a closed in darken cave; a nine room cave with one place of bathing; it was like a dark forest that I lived in, surrounded by steel pointed forks that could easily slice your skin to threads and deadly canines that stood tall as a toddler waiting to rip your skin to threads.

Did my grandmother really know my fate she had given me? Did she really care about me or my mom as she was trying to micromanage my mom life? Was she so angry with my mom that she could care less about my outcome, as she sat in Mark Tree and never once came to see me? Do she care about the woman that I would eventually become?

I don't remember her, but that is where my anger lies. She knew nothing about the demonic beast that rested inside of the woman that lived within the place I was forced to call home. I wasn't the only child living in the beast cave. Many was Fostered. Some like me, some not as fortunate as I would be, and others that was favored by the beast.

One thing for sure, if the beast was ever threaten by you, you would never stand a chance in hell, from the wrath that she would hand down on you. You see; I don't think you quite understand. I would never be favored by the beast and neither would my children. I taught them love and how not to get entrapped by the hatred and vile behavior of someone else.

The beast didn't start her terrorism with us; it's been here. I believe that it worsen over the years. No one would divulge her earlier years of life, her childhood; however, it wouldn't take much investigation to find out the darkness that ripped her soul to threads. Today, in the psychology world we have names for her behaviors.

She was Socio-pathic, Narcissistic, she suffered from a Personality Disorder, and she was schizophrenic. As a child, I would never know this; however, the White Coats knew and advised her to seek professional help immediately when she took me to the Psychiatrist as I tried to commit suicide, I defied the odds when I begin to fight back.

No one walked out of this cave if you broke the number one rule; "What goes on in this cave called home; stays in this cave." Family meetings were conducted if trouble transpired, An array of meetings were held in secret when you defied what the beast wanted. If you did not stand by her evil manipulative Jezebel rages; You were destroyed.

And she never would apologize for her behavior. The Break of Silence; would cause the beast to destroy relationships, family ties, and the worst, cause you to lose your life. See you don't get it. I had nothing to lose; nothing at all to lose. I had no one that would love me anymore, no one wanted me, I was in a place where I would never know what love mean.

You See, love is an action word. Some people feel as though material possession defines love. Money, clothes, shoes, houses, cars, and so forth; however, material items with no value means nothing to a child, where a simple hug is worth millions of dollars; where encouraging words and a simple I love you went further.

Love had become a rule of material possessions. Love was money and artificial items that would evaporate with time; The only love that Ava could hold onto is her mothers love, the memories that they shared together before Ava grandmother stole her life from her. The new world of love was Ava being held against her will, and raped.

No one ever told me that they loved me. Love to me was being beaten, slapped, bitten like a dog would bite raw meat as the beast would grab my tender skin and hold tightly until her teeth print was engraved into my flesh. Love was now the wrap tight arms of the rapist that would rip my tender vagina into a ripped burning fire.

Love was no longer about the good; love was survival. Surviving the beast and it's mates. Breaking the silence to heal my heart was the longest and toughest road that I had to travel down. No one to hold me and tell me that everything would be okay, and no one to protect me from the beast. I was A Lonely Stray, trying to hold on.

The beast was created in a woman shaped form with

sharpen teeth that often gnawed on chicken bones. You see, what everyone failed to realize is that I tried to make her love me; even if that meant doing wrong to impress her. I refer to her as a beast because no one human could ever be consumed with evil as she was. Her eyes would even change colors red.

This wasn't a natural behavior in a human being. I had never endured such evil. Breaking the Silence to heal my heart would bring closure to a life of darkness that I embraced as an escape. I begin to think that love was only filled with hurt and pain, sometimes I wondered why would people urn for such an intensed darkness that caused an abundant amount of pain.

People tell me often; "get over it!" My little sister made me feel like shit as she got older. Meanwhile, in my younger years, I became use to the beatings, the slaps, and the salt in the wounds as my skin buckled. I became use to being black-balled and holding my feelings inside and not releasing my emotions. I became use to not being liked or good enough.

But what I didn't get use to was the evilness that embraced this family that regardless of what I would do, if it wasn't something wrong that the beast wanted done, then it was never good enough. If you didn't have money you wasn't good enough. And you had to agree with what the evil demonic beast believed in or you would be done for.

The beast set me up! I was accused of being fass and out of control at an early age. However, I wasn't, I just wanted to be a successful entrepreneur and a professional criminal justice attorney. I had the stress of racial biases, this cave I was suppose to call a home, and the bullying from the students at school.

I could never call this my home, the violent nature and darkness that embraced every corner was not the silhouette that I was embraced up under. Love doesn't hurt like this. It doesn't cast the shadows of the grim reaper to ones heart and squeeze the very breath of life out of ones body changing their glow to gray or the day to night.

One day the beast set me up. You see, although I was called fat and ugly; I wasn't fat, and I have always thought that I was ugly due to my skin complexion; I was a caramel skin complected little girl, instead of a light bright, straight hair youngster like the beast wanted. Was the beast light skinned? No! This is the funny thing.

I guess it was time for the beast to have me broken in. I had really just begin to settle in after all the beatings that I had received from crying day after day and night after night to be back in the arms of my biological mother. It was only natural that I would long for her. Now it was time to tame me; It was time for to graduate.

I was not the only child in this household. All the children in this family that lived on Washington Street and their friends, would always be at the cave. This is the reason why I still think that this was a set up from the very beginning. It was only three permanent girls that was in the household at the time. Although Foster Care Girls would come and go.

But there were many boys that came through. The

beast sent me to her brother house to pick up the catch for the day, You see, on Saturday's, he would go to the lake and fish with the guy's. This was a well grown ass man with children and a wife. She sent me, out of all people to pick up the fresh catch of the day. I couldn't say no, I had to go.

I didn't know that he was attracted to the young, He had a love, a passion for the young, especially teenage girls. Today, I found this out the hard way. A beautiful Saturday, sunshiny day and everyone was doing their own thing. The beast sent me to pick up the fish that he had caught. I didn't think anything about it; I figured his family would be home.

When I arrived there, only his truck was parked in the driveway. I looked over to my Aunts house and her window was up. They lived side by side. I rung the doorbell, and he came to the door. He invited me in. I stood in the laundry room waiting on him; he told me to come to the kitchen. Still, not sensing anything negative, I was sooo, sooo Dumb!

The fish was in the sink and they were still alive. They were nice size catfish and one bass. The fish were flopping around in the water from the sink as if they knew today, their fate would be catastrophic. I was amazed at their behavior. I stood at the sink and gazed towards my auntie house. He walks up behind me.

I never realized, just how dumb I was until after everything was over and I begin to blame myself, I didn't know what was going on; yes, I was dumb and naive; "I Bet You Can't Get A Loose, He Say's?". I got a loose telling him that I need to go home. The rapist assured me that he had the beast in control. I never seen anyone around me control her.

He offers me some "Chips Ahoy Cookies!" This funny feeling comes over me like a mighty rushing wind on a hot summer day. I can't return without the fish. I can't shake this sickening feeling that aches my tummy. What was about to happen to me; a great fear took over my body. Seems as though he knew it. It seems like, like he became happier.

After telling him "NO," he offers me a hundred dollars; just to let him touch it, "Just let me feel it, I want hurt you, he says" as he grabs me tighter and won't let me go. I thought he was going to kill me and cut my body up and no one would know where I was. I tell him no; he say's he want hurt me; as he grabs me from behind and tighten his grip.

I was praying that his wife and children would walk in. No one came and no one called. His grip becomes tighter than before. I couldn't get away as he begins to grope my body. Now, I was for sure what this sickening feeling in my body was. I became weak, I couldn't feel my legs that was clearly attached to my body. I couldn't understand, why?

I didn't want his offers; not the cookies and not the hundred dollars, what I wanted to do is get these fishes and leave, before I got in trouble. His hand begin to touch my grapefruit sized breast as the left forearm wouldn't allow me to break his grip. His right hand leaves my breast and work to unbutton my tan skort.

It didn't take him long to get the first button undone.

He is beginning to become frustrated and attempted to go through the bottom and move my panties to the side. He undo my second button. You could tell that he was a professional at raping girls. He knew just what to do. Someone that hadn't raped a girl before, a child at that, it wouldn't have been easy.

He begin to touch me down there as I begin to try and fight him. I need an extra power surge of strength as I attempt to kick him from behind as he would not loosen his grip; it became tighter and tighter, as it becomes harder for me to breathe. He takes my hand and forces me to touch his man parts; his dick and balls.

It feels so nasty and slimy, as if I am being raped today, I feel it as if it was the first time. I had never touched anything like this. It's hot and big to room temperature. I don't know what to do. Another level of fear have set in as I begin to scream, he is sweating and smirking. He covers my mouth, tells me to stop screaming and he want hurt me.

I could only cry and ask him why; why was he hurting me? My smiles that I had earlier that morning, have turned upside down. The weather was beautiful, yet the clouds had taken over like a tornado about to touch down and clear everything in it's sight. I never thought this would happen to me. I never saw it coming and never saw the lustful stares.

A whole wife that he could have sex with, anytime he wants to, but he prefer to seek out young preteens and teenage girls. Like a zipper, my vagina rips, becoming nothing but an empty pussy, stolen at a young ripe age by the darkness of an empty satanic soul of evil, I feel it tear; ripping like cloth caught, snagged on a nail. I scream and cry, he don't care.

No one comes to my rescue me and no one attempts to protect me. He begin to strong arm me, he picks me up and tries to get me to his bedroom I cry and pray, cry and pray; I believe that God wasn't listening to me on that day, I believed that I was a curse from day one, no good would ever come to me, that is why all of these bad things are happening.

I wasn't a bad child, however, the beast made me out to be. Suddenly a knock on the door and I screamed and he laughed. He let's go of me, as I hurry to button my skort up and I run past my brother. What's wrong with you as he laughed; "he raped me, I screamed!" My brother laughed as if it was funny and he got the fish and brought it home.

I ran through the door of this place they now wanted me to call home. The beast asked me;"what took me so long?" She wanted to know, "Why was there dirt in the back of my head?" "He raped me," I replied. "Bitch you lying! Why is that dirt in the back of your head?" I told you, he raped me. With tears flowing like a rivers stream I cried!

Your just fass, that bitch put you up to say that, I'm going to teach you about lying. Just then the beast grabbed the big *Orange Outdoor Extension Cord. She begin to swing, I begin to scream, "I'm not lying, I'm not lying, he did! She beat me, she told me if I told anyone that she would kill me. Everyone ignored what she was doing to me.*

They turned their heads and never mumbled a word

for her to stop. They screamed at me, they were angry, my so called dad was angry; but they all was angry at me. Bitch go get in that water; she say's. She had made someone go prepare a clear chlorine bleach water for me to sit in after she was through beating me. The water was lukewarm.

I went to pee; the urine burned my vaginal area, he had split me open, I had gotten beaten, and now, I am forced to sat in this bleach water to remove the evidence that rest within my body and on my body. As I sit in this water, I could cry no more, Silence embraced my entire being. I couldn't talk and I could barely walk. All I could see was the darkness!

I no longer was in my body. I was broken to the very core. The little girl that once was, is now no more. The little innocent girl that wanted love and to fit in, she was gone. Her pain embraced tightly, as she entered into the dark world of depression. I didn't know who I was or why I was even here. Nothing mattered anymore.

I was confined to my room, I begin to embrace sleep, as I here the echos of the beast and her mates talk and degrade me. It was my fault that I was raped. I slept more, contemplating on how I would join the eternal darkness and rid myself of this pain and agony that had embraced me. They knew how he was and the beast made me pay for his sins.

I no longer desired to be around anyone. I hated this life. For days I grew more silent, I went deeper into this dark world. I walked like a drugged up zombie. Bitch, get in here and eat. I didn't want to eat and neither did I want to sit among them as they laughed as though nothing had happened to me. Why, why did he robbed me of my gold?

I would never be able to get my virginity back. As I tried to spend time with my aunt, I would see this mutherfucker that robbed me of something so precious and so important to me. Men would be sitting outside, and he thought it was funny to expose my tender young breast by jerking my half strapless tank top down. They laughed as I cried.

I wanted to kill him. I wanted to shoot him right in between the middle of his forehead, but I couldn't. Instead, I worked on ways to end my life. I hear the whispers as my name is being blown up. The beast would call on the phone, I would hear her calling me a lying bitch; "I'll beat her ass til the cows come home, and ain't no cows comin home."

She will never tell that lie again, she would say; I made sure of that. So, she knew what she was doing. And no one ever attempted to console me. Day's later, she did what she was good at; she attempted to talk to me, I walked out the room, but before I did; I would stare her down, with a look that says, "Your dead!"

She would give me money and tell me to go to the store for her and then, tell me to get me something. I never uttered a word. She would come to my bedroom, attempt to talk to me, as my back was turned, tears kissed my pillows with a silent cry, because I just wanted to die. I wouldn't eat, I would wait til heads were turned and throw my food away.

CHAPTER THREE

My Silence grew greater as the weeks and months passed me by. My only happiness came when the other children came through the foster care. I loved them, although I knew they were not going to stay long. I became attached to Jennifer. Her beauty was flawless. I held her and loved on her the way I wanted to be loved.

She was a bright complected infant. I assumed she was taken by the state from her biological mother and placed here. And then she could have been of a mixed race and that wasn't happening back then, so they gave her up. But she was a very beautiful little girl. She was the only Foster care child that not only I was attached to; everyone loved her.

She was spoiled by our hands. That was the only smile that I carried. She was the only one that brought a little sunshine to my life other than Sunshine herself. There were more *Foster Children* that filled empty spaces. She was the only one that didn't fall into the hands of the beast. She wanted to adopt Jennifer.

 For some reason the beast wasn't allowed too adopt her and that made me happy, because I knew the beast. The sunshine of this family was informed that someone had already did the paperwork to adopt her. My brief months of Sunshine was about to be removed. My temporary happiness was about to be taken away. Why would they do this to me?

Did they not care about my feelings? Obviously no one cared. Months later Jennifer was gone and we never heard from her again. I'm in Junior High School and I would never get use to this. My darkness had been deepened more than ever before. More rapes came as I became older. I knew to keep quite because everything remained in the closet.

I begin to act out as a result of my earlier years. I now have a new little sister that would be there. I was afraid to get attached to her, but I would be there to always protect her. I couldn't allow anyone to hurt her. The beast was good at hurting people especially children. She was a beautiful baby, not even a year old.

A beautiful mixed baby with slick cold black hair on her head. I would protect her like I tried to protect others; however, no one was there to protect me. You could tell that one of her parents were not African American. She looked like a little baby doll, except she would move around and she would cry, almost like a Baby Alive, but she was real.

I had the burden of school on me and living in a cave that I was forced to call my home. Although I couldn't remember many, I did have a few good times with sunshiny days, but it wasn't enough to pull me out of the deepened darkness and bring that sweet innocent girl of love that I was born to be, back to the starry lights.

I didn't have to worry about my little sister at the time and neither my little cousin. Both were beautiful mixed angels that I adored. However, I worried more about my little cousin than I did my little sister. My little female cousin lived right next door to the rapist, that made her more vulnerable than anyone.

I would spend the night down there as much as I could. The rapist is a career predator in the City of Jonesboro that allowed this faggot to get away with raping so many teens and molesting so many younger girls, that he knew who to strike and when to strike. They were as young as five years old. He would molest them.

He was sent to prison one time in his twenties for whatever reason. That was one of the top secrets. The beast became very angry when Sunshine would attempt to talk about it. They always would try to blame their darkness on other people. Concealing the truth did not make this fist of darkness a real man, he was still a piece of shit.

I personally think that his stay was for rape. His desire to have young girls wavered into late adulthood. You see, I wasn't the first and I am pretty sure I wouldn't be the last. However, it seems as though, I would be the only one to break the silence. For years no one would listen to me, no one cared and the beast made sure that I wouldn't talk by beating me.

His molestation; when he would pull down my tank tops and expose my naked grapefruit sized breast to the public and the men in the yard and the rape behind closed doors that stole my innocence from me seem not to bother anyone but me. His pedophilia behavior was not new. This career rapist use to peek through girls dressing rooms at school.

He would peek through windows and offer money to girls. Money that they were not accustom to and his favorite amount was a hundred dollars. Yes, a hundred dollars in those days were not a small amount. He would call the beast and lie and get money from her. Or maybe he wouldn't lie, since she would uphold him and his daddy in their wrong doings.

Many people wonder why Ava cannot break free from her rapes of this guy. Many wonder why her silence wasn't broken before now, or a few years ago. Well, the truth be told she did break it. She broke her silence many years ago and many times, but no one would listen. Ava was blackballed by the beast that she was forced to call a mother.

The beast turned everyone against Ava. She made Ava seem like the bad guy. She would tell the family that she was guided by one of the other girls that was in the family, that the beast didn't like. I never attempted to hurt anyone, and I wouldn't lie on them. The beast no longer like me or the other girl that urn for love at that house, I never knew why.

I figured that the beast didn't like us because we were the two that were liked by the beast mother; Sunshine. Her mother was my mother, and she taught me everything that I knew in the kitchen, how to be a woman, how to love, and also how to protect myself later in life. Sunshine was the only ray of consistent joy that shined through my darkness.

I thought I was a curse from my biological moms womb. I thought, at this time that I would bring bad luck to her, and that was the reason why I was there, at this cave like cage, the place I was forced to call a home. By this time the darkness that embraced my life was grim and each day was long. This was not my only rape; but this was the first one.

I remember; I remember one night while laying in bed. This place I called home, the voice of silence wreaked through the house like a bad plague. I was asleep on the top bunk with the only glare that peaked through the room was from the street light that shined through the black curtains that hung from my bedroom window.

I didn't like sunlight or any other form of light to be in my room. There was only one window that light kissed me from; aligned with beautiful thick rose bushes. I loved the rose bushes, although they were placed there for a reason. I begin to runaway! I would cut the screen from the windows after the beast would beat me and throw salt into my open cuts.

This one particular night, around two in the morning, I was awaken by a man wearing overalls. I was on the top bunk. The bunk beds were very thick and would hold many pounds. This man was midnight black. I didn't understand how he could by past the beast and get into my room. You had to enter into their room before getting into my room.

My stepdad face was always pointed towards the wall and the beast face was always pointed towards the opening of the door. She should have seen this man of tall statue enter into my room, yet her silence was greater; as great as my darkness that consumed my soul. There was no way you could sneak into the room where my so called guardians slept.

My stepdad would never harm me sexually. He was a good man, broken and trapped into this darkness. He loved the beast and often suffered from her hands as well. For some reason he would always come back to her when he would leave from being fed up from her abuse. One particular evening, I felt the heaviness of the black man inside me.

It wasn't enough that the beast gave me to her brother, it wasn't enough that my prized possession; my Virginity, that I wanted only my husband to have access too was negotiated, or the boys that came through the Foster Care, would play with my fragile and young tender area, and feel on my grapefruit sized breast and work to stick their dick inside me.

It wasn't enough that I was stolen from my mom at an early age, or deprived of my mothers love and having a relationship with my biological siblings, or just being treated and loved as a child and a teenager should have been, but the rapes and abuse was enough to stiffen the breath out of ones body. But now, I wonder if my biological grandmother knew.

I wonder if she knew just what she had done. From what I have been told later in life; my biological grandmother is the one responsible for my new home. I wonder did she really care, while she was attempting to teach my mom a lesson. The overall wearing, midnight black man climbs in the bed with me. I'm laying side ways he enters inside of me.

I no longer know who I am. I am no longer me. I became consumed with hate and vengeance. I no longer cared what anyone thought of me and really worked to either have the beast kill me or I kill the beast. I placed myself in deadly positions; another side of me, worked to avenge my honor and pain as the lonely loved sick little girl tried to escape.

I begin acting out at school in the classrooms of those teachers that were racist, mean, and nasty. I begin to target the bullies and hateful ass kids that wouldn't accept me and those like me that had no clue of what we had to endure in the hands of beast filled adults. I begin to protect the outcast like me, and I surrendered my body to those I thought cared. Why not?

Come to find out; I would learn that most didn't care; they only wanted one thing. And they would go back and talk about it with their friends; except for one guy, which I will talk about later. You see, I know that I am not healed, because the pain is still great. I write to be healed. I never write to hurt, I don't want to die and go to hell because I couldn't forgive.

As I write I listen to "Fear Not" soothing my soul as I take a moment to read Isaiah 41:10 and it gives me strength to continue to write. Why does it matter now; so many years later? It matters now because I am still trapped in my darkness, trying to escape, trying to find peace when only darkness continue to grab my soul.

I feel as though I continue to allow other people to walk over me, use me, and to enforce pain into my life. This is what I am use too. Being used up and tossed to the side, walked on like a worn out carpet sitting on the curb awaiting trash pickup on Thursdays. I just want to love and be loved. I am fifty-two, no one truly loves me.

I have accepted that those I grew up with will never love me because they don't understand the pain I have endured and neither have they walked in my shoes. They have always been taught that they were more than I could ever be. No matter how great my sacrifices were, they chose to be encamped and embraced with the poison that they were fed.

I never received justice for my pain, maybe this is the reason I held on and embraced the darkness for all these years. From the kidnapping, to the first slaps to the face, to the teeth that sunk deep into my skin, to the rapes, and outcast, no retribution for me in this life seem to ever rise to the fore front. No one would or could except the truth.

The only reason I do not name my rapist names is because of three of his children. Neither, should have to pay for his sins. One of his sons understood what I was going through. Little did they know, he was kind to me, even keeping me out of jail for retaliating on an abusive husband and a crooked cop as an adult; I loved him as a friend.

I could care less about the rapist. I did later on down the road try to treat him with respect, but that was difficult to do. Thinking back in time, I did confide in the only person that would listen to me, that would feel my pain and that could witness to the abuse that I was going through, because he saw the debris.

I found the only person at the moment that I could hold on to and that understood that I wasn't crazy. The only person at the moment that I wanted to enter into me and give me some comfort of what I thought was love. I had a boyfriend, despite what was allowed. They allowed me to be hurt and degraded. I could care less of what was allowed.

The beast allowed her brother and her dad to rape me; get me pregnant and then abort the baby by taking me to Doctor Frank James where he gives me a pill, reassures the beast that I would lose the seed that one of the demons planted inside of me and destroyed all the evidence by concealing the truth. Many people turned their nose up at me.

It was only discussed by three people; those were considered the heads of the family. I was sicken by what had happened; in two weeks she; the beast, had taken me back to see doctor James, this was to make sure the baby was dissolved. Needless to say, the only person that she had to answer too was God.

I remember in Junior High School; I would finally have someone to witness the debris from the abuse. One year while attending Douglas MacArthur; I was beaten bad by the beast. Previously no one cared to confront her, she was upheld in her wrong doing and she smiled with pride. Well, this particular day, I had been beaten and bitten by the beast.

I was lied on at school which wasn't anything new. One of the school bullies, that for some reason was attending this Junior High School, oppose to Annie Camp, decided to cuss out a teacher. However, the English Teacher lied; and said it was me. Not only did I get beaten for it, but I received a paddling for the lie.

Although later I was found to be innocent, Dennis Wegert smirked, with a simple apologize and Hornerker, with tears in her eyes, say's, I'm sorry, I should have listened. Before then, the damage had already been done. I was beaten at home before paddled at school. I was called out of class to the office one morning.

I knew what was happening, didn't care at the least. Mrs Davis was called into the office of Dennis, the Assistant Principal, where he sat and Mrs Summer's stood. Before getting a paddling, I had to remove my jacket; well, my sweater that the beast had forced me to wear. And this is where they saw the marks of the Beast.

My right arm was covered in bruises and right above my wrist, rested the beast teeth print engraved like a canines grip. I was asked to raise my shirt, Mrs. Davis couldn't stand it as she seen the buckling of my skin, my back filled with bruises and my arms covered with whelps as though I had been beaten by a slave Massa.

Tears filled their eyes and the eyes of Mrs. Summers. Mrs Davis worked to compose and gather herself. She asked me, "who did this to you; the woman I call mom!" Tear's filled her eyes, she was the counselor of the Junior High; she said, "I've seen an array of things in my life as a counselor, but nothing like this!"

She called me into her office after the assistant principal gave his slave driven speech to me. My head hung low, as he called my name. Taylor do you hear me; I raised my head, "Fuck You, I replied!" He said what did you say; "Fuck You and your slave enhanced speech, I replied!" Do you think you can hurt me, to late!

That day, I became someone else. As Judy, or Mrs. Summers struck with each lick as she paddled me, I begin not to care. I became zombified. Her licks didn't hurt, it turned into a rage. I didn't care about Wegert calling the beast and anyone else. I welcomed him to do so. Mrs Davis was a sweet elderly counselor that cared.

She let me know that she was bound by law to contact Social Services. I asked who were they and she told me that, "they protected children." I remember telling her; they couldn't protect me from the beast in the cave that I lived in. No one believed me, and no one would protect me. She assured me they would; she was wrong; I was right.

Not only did they allow me to be kidnapped from my biological mom, they allowed the beast to beat me like an animal being put down by the dog pound. And neither did they do anything about the rapes. I used this opportunity to tell them how my pussy had been ripped open by the beast brother and dad; yet, no one, faced retribution for their acts.

Ms. Dobbs was a worker for the State. She is the one that Mrs Davis said would protect me. Upon her visit, regardless of what the school officials witnessed, Dobbs allowed me to remain in the home. The beast told them I had to be tamed, I was fass, and was having sex with boy's; they left me there. I begin to skip school.

I begin to runaway and in the beginning I would stay hid out in cemeteries, where like minded and body people were. People like me, cold and dead; people in silence and darkness consumed and confined away from the walking and from the light. I was fitted for comfort there with them. I was at home when I was in the cemetery. No one ever hurt me.

One day I skipped school with my boyfriend. I spent the day with him in his dorm room. We were made to be together. He never forced me to do anything. He listened to me like no other, he comforted me, consoled me, and he assured me one day it will all be okay, the pain would be over. I wish I could have believed that.

He was the one person that would love me, that actually wanted to marry me, but that would never happen for me, because the beast would die before she would see me with an ounce of happiness. Dec was my boyfriend. I met Dec at Kroger's where he worked. He was a student at Arkansas State University.

Dennis wasn't from Jonesboro, he was just here going to school. I finally, one day after the beast had struck again, I had Dennis to pick me up early from school. I know what you all are thinking; "You were a little whore anyways!" No, I wasn't, I had one boyfriend, that loved me and I loved him. Thanks to the beast, I was not a virgin.

I had been raped, unwanted rapes by two grown ass men and some boys. No, I wasn't fass, and neither did I enjoy it, and I wanted for a change, to enjoy the feeling for once. I wanted to give my virginity up for once to someone that I felt appreciated it and not of the beast choice, but of my choice.

And Dennis was my choice.

For eight straight hours Dennis made love to me. Sweat poured off our bodies as he slowly treated my body as it had never been treated before. Afterwards, he held me as though I was a fleece blanket he used to cover up his chilled body with. He held me with his body pressed up against mine as if he would protect it from the pain I had endured.

Dennis would drop me off back at the school when it was time to return to the cave. One day, Dennis picked me up, as we laid there in the bed listening to soft sounds and just cuddling; Dennis asked me to marry him; although I said yes, I knew the beast wasn't going for it, and she would make sure that it would never happen.

That's exactly what happened. Dennis asked the beast, my guardian, my so called mom if he could marry me; "Her answer was, "No!" After Dennis asked me to marry to him; He disappeared. I pray nothing happened to him. He was no longer at Kroger's and no longer attending Arkansas State. What had the beast done? He would had never left.

I would never know, to this day, I try to find him, but have never heard from him. Things were never the same. Understand something, although I was in Junior High School, I was older than the majority of the students attending. You see, in order to keep my biological mom from locating me, my age and name was changed. I was two year's older.

The silly thing with all of this is that, it wasn't done in the proper manner; my transcript never was changed to fit their lies. You see, the beatings didn't stop, and neither did the abuse; emotional and neither mental. The rapes slacked up a little, and then eventually went away. But mentally, the rapes would effect my life for many years to come.

So, you can understand that my choices were limited like any other abused child. I didn't choose to be the girl, the teenager that I was turning out to be. Most holier than thou elderly people hated me, yet, didn't know the hell that I was enduring. I was expected to accept the abuse and deal with the deck that had been dealt to me; I didn't know how.

How do a child, ripped and raped from love, learn how to adapt to the marks of the beast? Especially, when the only two grownups around, one, for sure, could allocate what was really happening and they chose to turn their heads and closed their mouth. Pops, even if he cared, he would walk away as if he wore cataracts over both eyes, blinding him to reality.

He never protected me from the beast or the demons that rested right before him. When he was fed up with being abused, he could leave; when I was fed up with the rapes, the beatings, and the stoning, as a child and as a teenager, I was expected to "Deal with it!" I eventually snapped for quite some time. I couldn't tell you who I had become.

CHAPTER FOUR

For years I was forced to become someone that I didn't know. I became someone that was lost and confused. While everyone was laughing and throwing stones at me; I learned to conceal my darkness and eventually became lost in my own fears; creating my own world. From childhood to my teenage years, life was gone. I must search as an adult for me.

This is my transitional stage. At the time, I couldn't tell you the things that ran in my head, like a player headed for a home run on a baseball field or things that caused my head to pound like a meat tenderizing gadget kissing a juicy T bone Steak tendering each bite to satisfaction. They called me crazy, I just needed love, peace, to be held, and protected.

I thought that I was dumb, illiterate, and unable to excel in life. I was made to think that I had a learning development problem and was placed in Special Education. I actually went through SES due to a speech impediment issue when I was younger. I was in elementary school. I was told that I would be nothing, A whore just like my mama!

This is how the beast treated me and of course I begin to believe it. She told me that I would never amount to anything and that is why my mom didn't want me. I was the reason for everything that happened to me. That day, my entire life changed, once again. My life shifted in another direction and it wasn't for the good.

I vowed that the beast would never be able to control me again. I didn't care about the consequences that would be before me. Although the beast changed the year I was born illegally, everyone thought I was no older than fifteen; however, I was seventeen years of age. I was kept like a prisoner, caged and locked up.

I was in an Arkansas Alcatraz with barbed wire fencing with pointed edges. The side and back of the house was caged with a tall fence that you were unable to climb, decorated and heavily guarded with a German Shepherd and a nice size Great Dane. They would eat you alive if you even remotely tried to illegally enter or exit without permission.

No one on the outside understood my rage; however, I can no longer prove what I have attempted to prove for years now. What I would do, is protect the girls that came through this Cave as best as I could. I wasn't taking anymore beatings. I have been walked over so long, bullied at school and home, I would catch a charge if I have to.

What you didn't understand is the intensity of the violence that I was faced with. I became a gang member in order to survive the streets. I begin to fight back during the beatings. I couldn't take the feeling of that brown extension cord kissing my caramel brown skin, ripping the tender fragile pieces open with each strike.

I remember coming from church one Sunday, I had a wonderful time. I wore a black striped dress with hills. I was just about to come on my cycle and I didn't know it. I was drinking a Welch's Grape Soda that was icy cold. The weather was hot, it was a typical summer afternoon. The last thing I would think of but the first thing the beast would say is a boy.

I walked through the door of the house and caught a horrific cramp in my stomach, as I made it to the kitchen entrance. The cramp knocked me to my knees. The beast accused me of being fass and hit me upside the left side of my head with a bat. She then slapped me and continued to hit me as she says I had been with a man.

I wasn't thinking about a man and neither a boy. I enjoyed church, and that day was no different, However, that day made me never want to step foot back into another church ever again. The very exact so called Christians, had more hell and evil within them than the sinners had. The sinners were nice, loving, and most were calm

I found more love from alcoholics and crackheads than I did from church people and more love from the streets than I had in this so called holier than thou family of hypocrites. The lady that I looked at as my aunt was the only peace as a Saint I saw and the beast would mess that up with her lies and factitious stories. She begin to look at me as strangers did.

The well being of black children didn't matter back then just as these black children do not matter now to holier than thou rollers, to the State of Arkansas and to those that do not truly have the Love of God within them. He is the only one that will bring to light the lies and tales of the dark ones, like the beast and her comrades.

So, you see, my darkness begins as a fragile child, unable to make decisions for myself or I wouldn't have ever been in this position. My silence was justified and so was my darkness. It wasn't the wounds from those that had no knowledge; but the wounds and bruises of the lies that was told on me that effected me. For year's I concealed the truth!

The beginning of this abuse, lies, and torture begin simply because I wanted my biological mom and family. All I have ever wanted was what was mine, yet, I was forced to be what someone else wanted me to be. Why can I not let go of this pain and hurt; Because I want "Me" back. I have always been a loving and good person; no one cared to know, "Me!"

My childhood, the vulnerable little loving girl, the hurt, wounded, and abused teenager; only wanted her identity back, she only wanted others to love her as she loved or had the ability to love them. Ava longed for love so badly that she adjusted to whatever environment she was placed into. She even stopped loving herself, just to show others true love.

Ava learned to transform into the person that the beast wanted her to be. She knew when the beast was happy, because she would see the beast smile and hold a conversation with her, although Ava never received an "I love you" from the beast, the smile was soothing for Ava. It was hard for Ava to be mean, evil, and vindictive.

Inside, I was "A Lonely Dove," filled with a desire to be loved, liked, and belong. I lost myself while fighting to survive the vile of evil. My rage begin to show on surface. I became street when I needed to be street, Evil when I needed to survive, and loving when I needed to be loving. My body would shift, my head would pound; and I became no one,

I even became angry and folded a lot of times when the beast gave me an order. Why did I do evil things that she wanted me to do? The adults around me couldn't be as blind as they seem to be. You see, I know that I wasn't the only one that saw the attacks of evil that the beast ignited on those she didn't like. But they chose to adapt to her evil ways.

The beast would do crazy shit like, She would send me down to her sister house; have me to call back home and pretend to be another woman, just to jump on her husband. I remember asking him, why do he deal with this shit? He would weakly say, "She have to answer to God!" I would become in a rage, mad as hell at him.

I wanted him to stand up, be a man! How in the hell do he allow himself to be physically hurt and he ignore the shit she dished out to him. He wasn't doing her wrong. She didn't want him to see his mom without a fight, or his sisters and brothers, all except for one brother. She would start up shit with him and get her mom and dad involved.

Why did he allow her to be so vicious to him and he stayed? I would become angry as hell, but knew I couldn't say anything to anyone or I would pay for it. The children that came through the Foster Care was no different. Seems like, the beast knew that; No One Loved Us, and she could get away with the Maltreatment.

She would do evil shit that didn't make sense. She was truly deranged and everyone ignored it. Terra came through the Foster Care, a little dark skinned chocolate girl that had been removed from her home that was a victim of child abuse. She looked at me and smiled, as I smiled back at her. I grew fond of Terra.

The beast saw the love that we had for Terra and she worked to remove her swiftly. I begin to think that it was a sin to love people other than the beast. She would poor water into her bed and set her coat on fire, the coat that rested over Terra bed. Finally, the whipping that she was given didn't seem to work; she was guilty of nothing.

Well, she was guilty of only being a little girl that wanted to be loved, the beast deceit worked, and soon Terra was gone. Sunshine, thought the darkness was Terra; it was the beast. Only someone that was evil, could do the things to a child that the beast would do to these children, including to me. There was no way as a child I could understand.

Sherry was another Foster Girl. Sherry had been removed from her home just as many were. Sherry was a brightly complected teen that was different from most of us. In those days they referred to them as mentally retarded. Sherry was a sweet young girl that loved to smile. I thought she was safe from the beast. Truth is; No one was safe.

The key to the beast hatred was Sherry's disability. The beast hatred for Sherry showed through her actions. She use to sit at the table, and become in raged just by looking at her. If you looked into the beast eyes, you could see her transition, her anger, and her rage. The beast struck, she begin to lie on Sherry and then she would slap her for no reason.

Her beautiful skin turns red as fire as she wail with pain. Sherry was a good girl that never caused anyone an ounce of trouble. She might have been eighteen years in age but she was only around twelve mentally, if that. She couldn't really speak to be understood and was often ignored by people. Her disabilities was no fault of her own.

Sherry was my friend, she had a loving heart and just like myself, we just wanted to be loved and have a normal life. I remember one summer day, the adults and most children were sitting and playing outside as they talked and have a nice time. The beast and I, along with Sherry was in the house. I didn't want to be outside with the people out there.

Sherry was minding her own business and the beast walked into the room. The beast was acting strange, she kept looking out the door, she begin to laugh. She turned to me, she handed me a spoon. A tablespoon to be exact. I asked her for what, what was she about to do with it? She says to mind my own damn business. But to me; that was my business.

She slapped Sherry, jerked her shirt up; and placed that fiery hot spoon on Sherry's back. Again she wailed with pain. Her skin peeled off her back, like the peel of a banana getting ready to be eaten. I cried, I couldn't understand for the life of me, the pleasure someone would get out of inflicting pain on someone as sweet.

As if that wasn't enough, she mad her pull her clothes down between the living room and the dining room. She hit her and hit her over and over again. Sherry tried to pull her clothes up, yet the beast wouldn't allow her too. She opened the door and pushed Sherry out the front door and onto the porch. The rapist watched in amazement.'

I always wondered, why the rapist never touched Sherry, but he didn't. Many of you ask; "how do she know?" I worked to protect all the rest of the girls, because I knew what was going on. So, despite the craziness that we endured, Sherry went through some torture by the beast; but as far as I know she didn't endure the rapes.

You see, "Breaking the Silence," only help me mentally or psychologically most would say. There is no retribution otherwise for my pain, only to free myself. To heal is my primary focus to my broken heart, I have suffered long enough. I do not believe that I deserved the pain and suffering that I have endured. It's difficult to heal on top of current hurt.

I shouldn't have been ousted because of my desire to have my identity back. I shouldn't be hated by the mere beings that I believe to be the only family that I could hold on too. Sherry and I were not the only two that suffered through the abuse. There was Johnny which was a handsome lad. Of course, Johnny was not the type of child that the beast liked.

Johnny was another unfortunate soul that came through the torture chamber. I often wonder his whereabouts today. Johnny couldn't walk and neither could he talk. He was probably five maybe six. Another frail and beautiful soul. Johnny had been placed there like many, due to the abuse in the home. The State of Arkansas did not care about Blacks.

He was high spirited and like many of us, just wanted to be loved. These children were not problem children, like myself, we were just different from what the beast would consider normal. Johnny handicapped status made him unappealing to the beast. I knew that if anyone could help Johnny to walk it would be Sunshine.

She loved children and there was no one like her. It's like she had a natural gift for healing those that was turned away by others. Her silence was louder than any words that I've ever heard. She knew the beast that she had birthed into this world. I believe she worked to compensate the pain that her seed planted. But she never went against the grain.

Her love was unwavering. She loved her children unconditionally. And she loved other children as well. It's like she tried to make everyone happy, She was loyal to her family and she stood by them despite what they had done, but she worked to bring sunshine to the hurt and despair. She often set in silence, with her bible opened in front of her.

When her son went to prison, she blamed others for his fate. They set him up, she would say, as she continued to protect him in his wrongdoings. Her daughter, the beast, had split personalities. One minute she was fine and the next minute a demon would rule her every existent. She blamed her violence and hatred; her daughters rage on diabetes.

Well, many would never believe that the beast would go this far and be this evil. What she does next to Johnny could be the worse cruelty that any human being could ever endure. It was already bad enough, she would slap him around just because he was different, but since that didn't get rid of him, well she went a little bit further. Too Far!

She decided to give him a new entree' for a snack. Sunshine worked with Johnny, exercising his legs day and night. He begin crawling and then soon after walking. He was so excited to be able to move around like everyone else. It was an exciting day for all of us that loved Johnny. The beast saw danger; she saw the love for him.

Everyone was entertaining themselves in other rooms. Sunshine, was in her room with her closet of darkness, Jay was in my room watching television as usual and everyone else was doing their thing of the evening. I walked into the dining room and stepped around the buffet that rested against the wall close to the bathroom.

I was stunned by site; it was sickening, the sickening that my eyes would see before me. The beast was feeding Johnny her feces or his feces one. She smeared it all over his mouth as if he was enjoying it. I seen him shake his head and try to move back. His potty was a little wooden frame pot with a white insert and trim.

Sunshine listened to the beast as if she was telling the truth; as she yelled in disgust. She should have known that Johnny didn't do that if just for a moment, if she had of just stop and looked. She knew he wouldn't do that to himself; Yet, the words of the beast, her words pierced my ears, because her lies echoed as she spoke.

I moved back, as mother and everyone came into the room. The beast said that he; Johnny, was eating his defecation. He was eating his own bowel. I blurted out, "she lying!" She slapped me so hard, I stood there drew my fist together and thought about hitting her in her freaking mouth. I stopped, knowing if I had of hit her, it wouldn't be nice.

I knew that they would all dog pile me. Soon after that, Sunshine returned Johnny back to the Child Services people. I couldn't help but cry when they picked up Johnny and carried him away. Hopefully, Johnny would find a better and more peaceful home and escape the abuse. Maybe, just maybe now, Johnny would find a loving home.

Maybe, Johnny, would be better off than most of us would be. Maybe, just maybe, Terra, Sherry, and Johnny would find a normal home with adults that would treat them with the love and respect they deserved. There were many others that would come through and would endure some type of suffrage from the beast during my time here.

Gwen was another mahogany girl that came through this cave of pain. She was between twelve and thirteen. Gwen was coming from another facility. Another victim of the Arkansas Child Protective Services System. She was quite, shy, and wanted what all of us lacked. This road was never easy for neither of us; love is all any of us desired.

Many people will never understand. When children are suffering from the pain of misuse and abuse, trauma or emotional distress, a child must fight to survive. This is what Ava and Gwen, along with other abused and misused unloved children must endure on a daily basis. The lack of love can drive you insane, especially if you already have issues,

The inability to embark on a positive environment makes it almost impossible to recover from one pain to the next. How do we escapee the toils of evilness sent to destroy our vulnerable and fragile mere existence as young tenderloins? How would the rapes, physical, mental, and emotional abuse pave Gwen and Ava's future in this life?

Although all the rest of the girls that entered into this cave had left, Gwen, Lynn, and Ava wouldn't leave until they turned legal. They were stuck. Lynn had no problems whatsoever, they loved her, but Ava and Gwen was not liked at all. When Ava would try to tell the truth, she was made out to be a liar by the beast.

Ava, wasn't like other children and neither teenagers. She wasn't one that copied what others would do and follow behind them. Ava, had her own thoughts and desires. She never hated others because someone she knew disliked the person and neither was her relationship conformed to adjust. If you treated Ava right, Ava would love you regardless.

Ava cried when she saw others hurting. No one had a heart in her environment like this girl; this made an array of people fear her. Sunshine, on the other hand, knew that Ava was unlike others. She was a peculiar child that had a purpose, even though Sunshine never protected Ava from the beast.

She would one day witness to Ava about an event.

She didn't know why God had placed Ava here; she knew time would tell. One day she sat Ava down with the beast, The beast was in her human form at the time. They begin to reminisce on earlier times; apparently when Ava first arrived in Arkansas. She begin to tell Ava about a mysterious light that awaken them.

This light shinned so brightly over Ava head. The light caused the beast to scream; it awaken everyone in the house. Sunshine says that the light glowed like none other. However, the light was like none other. It just shinned over Ava and no one else. As they looked, trying to figure out what was going on, Sunshine noticed the halo that was there.

Sunshine, told Ava, I knew from that point on, that you were a special child. You would never be like anyone else. We couldn't explain what was happening, Sunshine said, but in my spirit, I knew it was a divine purpose and that you would be misunderstood by many people. From that day forward, your life would change; you Ava was protected.

No one is perfect and we all go through trials; however, there are always reasons why we endure our trials and some more than others. You are a blessed child and something is protecting you. You will not understand, but you must remain in church. Now, as much as I wanted to believe, I had the faith of none. Even when the Angel visited me.

CHAPTER FIVE

After this talk that Sunshine, Ava, and the beast had together; Ava became more confused and the beast became more determined to destroy Ava. You see, the churches in the beginning that Ava was dragged too, wasn't the right spirited churches. The demons that Ava faced was from the soul of one person and not who the beast would use for her lies.

The beast would lie as though Gwen put Me up to the things that I would seek help for. Never once did Gwen ever have anything to do with my battles; How could she, when she had her own monsters hanging on her shoulder's. It should have been enough. Gwen have never had an easy life. In the beginning, when Gwen first arrived, you could see hurt.

Gwen biological mother was very young when she had her. She was only thirteen. I don't quite know how she got into the Foster Care system, but she did. The Cave of doom was not the first place Gwen was shipped too. She came to this part of Arkansas from a country town called Camden. Life wasn't easy in Camden for her either.

Most people don't realize or choose not to realize the pain that a person endure directs their path; either for the good or for the bad and it often causes an array of emotional and mental battles in ones mind. Mental trauma can cause a perfectly normal child to snap and become his or her own worst enemy.

The trauma can be suicidal physically, mentally, or emotionally. Sometimes she would sleep in the woods to avoid some of the treatment that she was enduring. I overheard the State worker talking about her. Just like myself, she had found herself a safe-haven. That was our connection. She had the woods and I had the cemetery.

That's right, I had the cemetery. We had to find a "right now survival plan!"She had been raped more than once. I believe that is how she ended up here in the cave. I hated it for her, because I knew her pain and distress. Little did she know in the beginning that, this place would be no better than where she left.

I don't know about how bad she was beaten, but I'm pretty sure beatings came along with the rapes. At least that's how it worked for me. Gwen was known as the "Crazy Girl."She really wasn't crazy, she was hurt. She was in pain and seeking love. The beast hated her, because mother wanted to make Gwen her own.

She didn't want to send Gwen back to the dungeon in which she had came from. She saw that need for love in Gwen and she wanted to give it to her. The beast transition from that so called sweet lady that everyone thought she was, to that beast, that I knew she was all along. Picking and choosing when to come out and just who would see her.

The beast would play the victim for others that would show her empathy. The beast was in full force. She had to get Gwen out the way; however, she didn't know how. The beast was creating and devising plans to have Gwen removed before the adoption came through. She use to lie so badly on Gwen, just to see Sunshine whoop her.

Sunshine was from the old school. She didn't abuse you, however, those old fashion woodshed whippings, would make you remember when you did wrong. I didn't mind her whippings, I appreciated them down the road. She didn't use cords and brooms. And when you thought you were to big for whippings, Sunshine would hog tie you down.

I appreciated Sunshine's discipline. Because of her guidance, I am the woman that I am today. I've never been perfect but I am not who the beast made me out to be. Gwen finally moved away from Arkansas; which was the best thing she could have done. Why? So she could have a brand new life without the debris from the beast.

The beast destroyed her name beyond gentrification. The beast would do stupid shit like go and grease her cucumber with lard and lie on Gwen as if she was responsible. She would place flour or talcum powder into paper and when there was no one looking, the beast would throw it on the front porch.

A short while later, she would put on a great drama, causing a major scene. The beast would throw a fit, saying that Gwen was trying to fix her. I couldn't dislike or hate Sunshine, who would you believe, the new kids on the block, or your biological daughter that you reared from birth after carrying her through pregnancy term.

The truth be told, the entire thing was the beast doing. How do I know; because I seen it for myself? She would grease the cucumber with lard, and the powder substance she would sprinkle flour or other substance in paper. Sunshine would believe the lies. And if I hadn't of seen it for myself, would I have fallen into that same web of belief.

Gwen felt the hate from the beast, she would often be whipped for no reason at all. She begin to act out. Gwen hadn't had any help learning how to deal with the trauma that she had endured in the past and the trauma she is going through here in this cave. The beast tactics did not work and Gwen was a permanent residence here.

She did not have it easy and neither did I. When we had family gatherings down at Cheryl and her husband house, she would hear the beast talking ill about her and she would cry and storm out the house. Soon, Sunshine would take her to a white coat doctor and get her some help. Like myself, that didn't last for long.

This is what people failed to understand, We did not work to be a problem to anyone. It is difficult to remove hurt and pain from a person's life, but it is impossible to mend a broken heart when no one replaces the love that was lost. A child is fragile, vulnerable to losing people such as a parent or sibling, great help will be needed to win.

Every time I attempted to do right, the beast would attack, her attacks were like the venom of a rattlesnake, lethal and often fatal. You have read about bits and pieces of the abuse and rapes that I have sustained as well as the trauma of others that came through this household. No one understood this and was quick to stone us.

My dreams had been crushed and I genuinely thought that I was dumb as a bag of bricks. Why try when I would be nothing anyways. I didn't understand, but I conformed to what my fate seem to be. Later Gwen and Lynn left and there were no more Foster Care Children in the home. I was alone, no other girl's around my age lived here.

I became very promiscuous, very angry, and hostile. I felt like, since I had no choice of being a virgin on my own, I might as well give to someone that could possibly love me. After my boyfriend Dennis disappeared with no trace, I was very angry. I knew he did not leave on his own and I would never know what happened. To this day I can't tell you.

I am lonely, angry, and mentally exhausted. No one understood what I was going through. The State of Arkansas didn't give a damn about the truth, the rapes, the beatings, and mental anguish. They allowed these things to happen to us and I feel as though they owe us dearly; they owe us our life back. If they didn't know before, I brought out the truth.

They allowed our identity to be changed, the year we were born changed along with the name, city, state, and even our social security numbers changed. Arkansas will jail us, place us in prison; Federal Prisons at that for tampering with Social Security Numbers and Identity. They call it Identity theft; however, they never once charged them.

We are held accountable, red flagged, stripped of our rights, and pay for our freedom; yet the adults that I was around, wouldn't have to pay for their actions as they robbed, killed, stole, and deceived young souls, innocent children, and vulnerable parents. When will they face their retribution and pay restitution for their actions.

You see, there is proof that they know, remember the lady, Ms. Dobbs and Douglas MacArthur, remember Summers, Davis, and Wegert, they were just the few witnesses that could verify the abuse; not to mention the Psychiatrist that could authenticate the mental illness of the same woman/beast that called herself my mother.

I became part of the bastard nation, at least that is how I felt and no one at that time was there to tell me any different. Now, No one really wanted to know the truth, inside or outside of this family. It seems as though as long as life was good for them; those around me, that's all that matters. This wouldn't end now. Every one was better than me and my kids.

Many saw us as bad and crazy; however, could you survive the torture that we went through for years? How would you feel if your daughter, a fragile innocent child had a grown man and men; ripping her virgin self to pieces? Feeling him, forcing the head in her small tender area. There were prostitutes in this town and whores that would have loved it.

A grown ass man; actually getting a thrill from feeling the insides of a little virgin girl with much pleasure. How would you feel if knowing your child was stolen from you, praying your child was in a safe haven, but finding out after not only being raped, but beaten and abused time after time, again and again with no remorse? No one to love you?

Now, your told that the purpose that you were taken was to protect you from your biological mom. However, you find out that the only reason you are here is to be a pawn on a chess board. To basically allow them to hurt you mentally, physically, and emotionally, killing your very soul. Making your existence the silhouette of darkness.

CHAPTER SIX

Ava never thought that she would survive the trauma that she endured. Many times Ava was lied on to the extreme. From being a runaway to contemplating on murders, Ava begin to think harder on how to escape. I still couldn't escape the rapes and neither the beatings. It never mattered where I would be, I became a rape target.

One adopted boy followed lead of the rapist. Jerry, was lost and confused. He was placed in this family just like all the rest of us were. The rapist kept him. The rapist was not a good leader or role model for anyone. He had no morals and definitely no values. The words in his eyes spoke louder than the sounds of a damsel in distress.

I don't know what all went on down there in that den of sin; it was dark! They were allowed to drink alcohol as children and skip school when they chose to do so, the rapist didn't care. It seems as though, the rapist, made it okay for those boys around him to defy the odds. I was good at observing people at this point in my life.

You see, in order to survive I had to learn those that was around me. Nothing around me was normal at all. In abnormal situations, you must be able to identify in order to keep your sanity. I watched the rapist often. Especially when he decided to bring his sick ass up to Sunshine house. His visits were dark, grim, and evil.

I believed in my mind, he would come up there and set things up with the beast and then go see everyone else as he sit and watched me; I was the only one left there that was a female that he can take control over sexually and it would be okay. The walk of a mere fragile child, what was more sicker than that.

He had no remorse when it came to his behavior. Now, how would you handle this situation? Every time I turned around I had to learn how to survive. It was okay for him to brush his nasty ass up against me or walk by and grab my nipples as if I was a cow ready to be milked. I, begin to runaway!

I was called a whore for so long, I was told that I was going to be a bitch like my mom, and I was told that I would never amount to anything by the beast or the woman

I called mom. I had heard this oh too often. However, no one else heard those bitter and hateful words. It was only me, yet your pretty little ass thought I should, what?

Did you think I was going to continue being the useless pawn on the chess board? Did you think that I would remain a victim of free enterprise where he would rest his massive weapon of destruction and continue to make his career, town, and community rapist weekly deposits? Rape and neither is molestation okay.

Did you think that I would never gain my independence; while I was being beaten like a runaway slave? Well, this time, however, for some reason, it just didn't sit well with me, It seems as though my soul left my body. To hear her say that, "I was going to be a bitch and a whore just like my mom."

Her words echoed in my ears; I would never amount to anything, that day, I vowed to never be able to be handled again. I thought back to the lies, deceit, rapes, and beatings. Not anymore! This time I was bold about what I was and wasn't going to deal with anymore. I was at the end of my ropes, I couldn't deal with this

With tears in my eyes, I stood there, as she stood in the doorway of her bedroom and I looked in her eyes boldly on this Saturday and let her know; "You have no more control over me, I said to her!" That day I would think back to my pain. I thought back to the rapes, the degrading words and each strike with that brown and extension cord.

I thought back to that first rape and that big thick orange extension cord that cut deep and those words; I will kill you if you tell anyone this lie. The first thing I told her is that, "And that's exactly what I am going to do, be a "BITCH JUST LIKE MY MOM!" I worked daily to uphold my words. My mind was all over the place.

Jerry, attempted to rape me while we were on a trip to Mississippi, the rapist got up and jerked him off of me, and smiled. A child learned behavior comes from the parents or guardians in which they are reared upon. In order for children to be productive and positive; they must be around positive pillars of the environment. This was not the case for us.

They set Jerry up, I believe, but it wouldn't be the last time. The rapist perversion and lack of belief in a higher being have being shown through his behavior. I couldn't help but to think back to the very first slap in the face. I thought back to my moms hug and embrace, that lost, pitiful look that rested within her and ripped her soul away.

Mom was hurt and I truly know that she loved me. This woman had taken the only love from me that I knew was genuine. They never wanted me; Do you know how that feels? Can you imagine not being caught up on material earthly possessions, but just want to be loved by someone? Do you realize the importance of true, real, and genuine love?

It is not love when a child is bullied by adults because you want to do right, but forced to draw a neon light in the dark. All the bruises and bite marks on me as if I was attacked by an animal, the emotional and mental distress was heavy. The abortion that she had done to me and the abuse that Terra, Johnny, and Sherry endured; it all hit me on this day.

No love, the abuse of extension cords kissing my fragile soft skin, The words against the only love I've ever known. The hatred I saw in the beast eyes never left my memory. The vile actions to me and the other children that thought there would be protection and comfort would come through this place. And that first rape, that very first rape!

That very first rape, the beating, the trauma it brought; it all proved to hunt me for years down the road. I begin to runaway and would stay gone for days. I knew I had to hide out and couldn't allow anyone to find me. Sometimes those nights in the cemetery became cold, dark, and lonely; yet the most peaceful place that I had in my life.

My life had spanned out of control. After years of no help, and no love; I was never the same anymore. I tried so hard to be more than I was, but I just couldn't get passed the trauma. I begin to fight back with all I had. I no longer cared about the consequences, because I was no longer me. I was someone trapped in a body that I didn't even like.

I looked in the mirror, I didn't even know the girl that stood before me. Who was the girl in this body? I can't remember an array of my teenage years because it was no longer me. I didn't mind fighting, having sex, popping uppers, smoking weed, and telling you just how I felt. I didn't care what anyone thought of me and I would do whatever I chose.

When the woman I called mama would go to beat me, I no longer stood quite. This reaction from me would cause her husband to jump into it. He would cuss me out and sometimes jump on me. He never knew what anything was about, and he chose to listen to her. What he should have known is that she was a liar and was very manipulative.

It wasn't okay for her to lie and abuse children the way that she had done. It wasn't okay for her to spun evil with a smile, yet he had no problem with walking away with a blinded eye like the darkness without any light. I could no longer kiss the silhouette of the angel that rest inside me. I couldn't find her as hard as I searched for her she had left.

I begin to runaway more frequently. I begin to fight back more frequently. I wasn't a lovable site, especially at school. I would normally move around like a silent shadow stuck in the mist. I would have no conversation for anyone, unless you were kind. I launched at evil as though it was a rocket launched into space by NASA.

I begin to smart off at the teachers, I would sometimes walk out of class and go rest in the bathroom in order to breathe. I loved band and choir, although I didn't care for the instrument that I played. It became boring, I wanted to play the Bass Clarinet, the Saxophone, and the Drums. I loved choir, singing, allowed me to express myself off paper.

The days became long, and the summer even longer. I remember our math teacher, He was going through a rough time in his adult life and often brought it to school and would take it out on his students. He would get smart, yell, and threaten the vulnerable students. I had a long day at that place I called home and it wasn't a good day for him with me.

I went to school and Mr. Lewis started in. I was put out of his classroom because I wasn't going to allow him to attack anyone in our class because he had personal problems going on in his life. He was an adult; how did he think I felt as a child, dealing with everything that I was going through and had been going through for years?

I decided one day to put him out of his own classroom. Not the way that you may think, but I wanted him to feel a dose of his own medicine. He thought it was funny and cute when he picked on us. He would sometimes call me out in the hallway and give me this bullshit ass lecture that I didn't care to hear. He didn't care how he dressed or looked.

One day me and my friends decided to give him a gift package. We thought that he couldn't afford to keep his personal hygiene up. We stock piled deodorant, mouthwash, shampoo, and other goodies in a gallon freezer bag and we sneaked into his classroom and placed it in his desk. We knew he would go into his desk for a pen and would see it.

Instead of being appreciative that we didn't place him on blast, he became very pissed. Although he didn't say anything, he took it out on my cousin. I seen his tear drop and set out for vengeance. The next day, I brought a melted snicker bar to school. I had a couple of my friends at that time watching for him, I meant that we would have a substitute.

I smashed the soften almost melted snicker bar up in a plastic sandwich bag and then dumped it into his chair. I made sure that the chair was completely up under the desk; when he came through the door, walked to his desk, I struck his attention. I begin to ask him questions that really wasn't my business, but at that time; I could careless. He fell for it.

I wasn't mean to everyone, just those that were mean, evil, and racist to those that I loved or were considered outcast. All I had was my friends and a few that called themselves my family; I would protect them at all cost. No one protected me. I did apologize to Mr. Lewis, and later I found out that he had a nervous breakdown.

Just like Mr. Lewis did not know what some of his students were going through; neither did we understand and know what he was going through. I later felt bad, and really did want the best for him, so, when he returned to school, spoke to me like a human being and we ironed out our differences, I spoke to the others and we laid off of him.

I didn't like the gym teacher with her dike looking ass. She was mean and hateful unless you were one of those fancy volleyball players. Most was white of course. Mind you I was not a racist, although I lived in a racist environment. One day, we had a full fledged riot at school. This came after the school decided to play racial movies.

I remember the movie roots that showed the ownership of slaves and the depiction that black people were beneath whites. I felt as though I was living a nightmare. I begin to cry, relating to the whips that kissed the skin of the blacks on this movie. I would return to school and have some of the white kids call me or someone else a nigger.

As if that wasn't enough, they spray painted our lockers with white spray paint. It read in bold letters, "KKK," I became furious, angry, and enraged. What pissed me off worse, is that the principals knew who had done it and did nothing about it. I started that riot. Changing KKK to BKKK, which meant the "BLACK KLU KLUX KLAN!"

Although it never changed their ways of thinking because that is what was in there hearts; they knew that we were not afraid of them and that we would fight back by all means. They knew that I didn't care and I was very violent. I could be extremely evil if I chose to be. Most people knew that I didn't want to be mean but this meant war.

But the person that I would become was one that many loved to hate. I could be the most loving person around, however, I could be provoked and I would become the most wicked. I didn't know how to get myself back. I was tired and weary. I enjoyed playing basketball, it would give me some time away from the evil that surrounded me at home.

This wasn't the person that I chose to be or the life I wanted to live. Home life didn't get any better. I missed my biological mom daily. One thing that I always knew; I knew when I was going to be beaten or raped. I would become nauseated with sickness, my stomach would turn like the wheels on a bicycle.

I started leaving and staying gone. I was allowing the streets to eat me up. The love of my life had disappeared without a trace. There were no goodbyes, phone calls, or letters. I would sometimes stay gone for weeks at a time, other times for days. Sometimes, I would be nearby and see the polices looking for me, I never bulged.

Other times, I would be hiding out when they knocked on a door and I was inside and didn't want them to find me. One evening, I was hid out at my uncle's house and heard their bullshit threat. They didn't scare him and they didn't scare me. I just didn't want to get anyone in trouble. I could breathe for a moment not being in that house.

I watched the beast become a mother to my beautiful sister. I seen how she loved my handsome brother, and I seen how she made me the total enemy to even them. Her lies and deceit; the ways she manipulated them and they believed her; cut me like a two-edged sword. See, when you read this, you may say I'm all over the place; I am because of my memory.

I lost my memory in order to survive. Blackouts is what they call them in the professional community. A coping mechanism in order to survive trauma. I remember running away from this place and ending up at, what they called the Youth Home. I didn't care, because this was a peaceful place for me regardless of the fact it seem to be a kiddy jail.

Regardless of what you did or where you went, and even with whom you went with, you always had a smart mouth ass guard with you. A worker in this facility would stand and watch over you if you earned points to go out on the weekend. Those that were in school would go to school from there or they would attend school at the facility.

I remember Pops coming to visit one day. He would ask if I was ready to come home. I let him know how I felt. I didn't want to be in such darkness that brought evil out of me. No one loved me, I was stripped from my mom just to be stepped on and abused. No one loved me, and it showed. He tried to convince me that I was loved; that the beast loved me.

I didn't want to see her or have anything to do with her. While I was in the facility, we earned money, and each Friday and Saturday we would go out to the skating rink or to the movies. We had fun and I enjoyed myself. The counselor would call me in and talk to me frequently. Unlike the majority of the kids there, I was there because I wanted to be.

The other youth in the facility was court ordered. One evening, we were getting dressed for bed. I wanted my hair cut, a new style; I wanted a shag; this was the new style wave for this era. There was a girl that everyone assured that she was a professional. To make a long story short; she messed up my hair and I kicked her ass. Yes, I went overboard as usual.

I couldn't control my anger at all. I didn't think about, it was hair and it would grow back; That's the only beauty to me that I possessed. The girls in our dorm knew how I felt about my hair, so, I believed that she messed my hair up on purpose. I had no remorse on busting her head; sending her to the hospital; I became the very evil that I detested.

No one knew the anger I carried inside of me. The facility manager no longer wanted me there. I saw the woman that I called mom walk through the door. She was there for a meeting with the director. Although I didn't leave with her at that point, I was picked up a few days later by Pops. Things went okay for awhile, then back to her degrading ways.

We were forced to stay in church which became very tiring. I long to again blend in and be apart of something called love. No one understood my behavior. It wasn't in my heart to kill and I became to afraid to fight females. It wasn't because I was afraid of them; it was because I feared that I would kill them. I felt this way because of the pain inflicted.

The rage that I took out on the girl that messed my hair up was not justified as I think back today on it. It was the hurt and pain that had been bottled up inside of me for many of years. I could not separate the difference. I remember the woman of evil hating my hair and that is all I could think about at that time.

I remember the beast hatred of my hair, it caused her to change my color from sandy brown to jet black. That was not my color and it was not my style. It caused her to place chemical relaxers in my hair and change the texture of my natural wavy and curly hair. She placed Gerry curls in my hair and often told me how nappy my hair was.

It wouldn't be until I became an adult that I would find out that I did not have a bad grade of hair at all. It was just the opposite. Everything about me to them was wrong and I was trapped in that darkness the rest of my teen life. I became my own worst enemy. Regardless of what was placed in front of me, I couldn't see the benefits only the darkness

All that echoed in the back of my head is that I would never amount to anything. I was going to be a whore just like my mom. The rapes; my tender fragile vagina turned into nothing more than a used up pussy, waiting for the next man that wanted to widen it and violate the innocence of my gold mine. I didn't choose this, this life was chosen for me.

The summer months was long and miserable for me. I became depressed and uninterested in anything. I would go to church because I didn't have a choice. School didn't interest me because of the stones thrown by the teachers, my peers, and the adults that surrounded me. I was a member of Upward Bounds; a teen group that worked to strengthen Youth.

This didn't work, although I enjoyed it. Nothing worked, because I was in pain, I was hurt, and I was unloved. How could anyone expect me to change and I was in this battle on this journey alone? I begin to be the whore that I was told that I would be. I was aware that no one would love me, I was ugly, and according to them, I was fat.

In my eyes, the only pleasure that was there for me is allowing the cute and popular boys to use me up, just as the rapist. To allow the pain of the older boy's to enter into my used up pussy. No, I wasn't like the other girls that had a choice if they wanted to give up their virginity, mine was given up at an early age. Taken by an old wrinkle dick bitch.

I didn't have a choice in this life, yet, you judged me as an out of control teenager. I was like the bitter middle of a head of lettuce, undesirable. For years I was like a wandering abandon pet, searching for scraps of love and no one is feeding the strays. Now that I don't give a damn, your hatred is on pause. I don't know how it feels to be loved.

Love is not about material possessions, but about the actions of the emotions of kindness and heartfelt feelings. Because of your cruelty, I can't go on; Ava decided. The last straw, the last rape, the last beating: it all pushed me over the edge, according to Ava. I just couldn't do it anymore. I am now in High School and I still was treated like shit.

I loved high school. I loved most of my classes; however, the trauma that I was enduring, the hatred, the loneliness, and the low self-esteem wouldn't allow me to concentrate. Even the principals were different here. I tried to keep going. I wasn't even skipping school anymore. I was trying to play basketball and stay in band; I couldn't.

The last straw, the last episode, the last crash; caused me to give up. I wanted more in life, but again, I really felt as though I was cursed, and I really felt for the first time that my job was to please a man and make others happy. This life was not about me and I had to understand that regardless of what was around me. I would never be happy.

CHAPTER SEVEN

There was only one woman that saw something in me that I would or could never see in myself. She is the very exact reason I even passed and came to the high school. She jerked me up when I was in Junior High and wouldn't allow me to give up. She gave me a chance and her belief in me would remain there when all else failed.

I dropped out of High School. I was tired of the abuse and degrading acts towards me. I was tired and fed up with the lies and manipulation that often consumed and filled my ears. I couldn't deal with it anymore. The beast had everything she wanted and that was my little sister and my brother. She didn't want me, her and everyone else wanted my older sister.

I was going out with an older boy that wasn't from here. He moved down here from Memphis, Tennessee. He was working for Indian Mall Security. Now, as I think of it, I wasn't in love with him, but to me it was the only love that I would know since I was with DEC. At this time, he is the only one that cared. I would get his car when he would go to work.

Just like Dennis, or DEC, he wanted to marry me and the beast wasn't going for it. It wouldn't matter to me anymore what she wanted, but he had to have their permission. I kept telling him, I was of consenting age; yet he still had to have the permission of the very exact woman that hated me. You knew she wouldn't consent.

The beast liked Lonnie until he wanted to marry me. She would ride with us to church, and wanted him to take her places. I stayed with him most of the time, not having to deal with the trauma until the beast would become angry. Many didn't know that I wasn't as young as they lied and said that I was. I was actually two years older.

They had lied so much and so hard on me that I was made out to be a liar. I knew who I was, but couldn't remember my name. My name wasn't the name that they were calling me. I wasn't from where they continued to lie like I was from. I dropped out of school because I wasn't about to deal with the abuse anymore.

What they didn't know; I was pregnant. I was pregnant with what I thought or remembered to be my first child. Lonnie, wanted to do the right thing. He felt it was important for us to be a family, but would need their permission in order to be blessed. I knew what she was going to say, although everyone else said yes; she would lie and put on a show.

He pleaded with her, but she didn't cave. I now was her baby, bullshit; she just couldn't see me being happy and she couldn't see anyone else loving me. She wanted to continue to control who would enter into this once innocent vaginal torn pussy. I was so angry, so destroyed, but she; the beast was not ready for what was about to come.

The lies would unveil before everyone around. Not all of them but the most important one. Lonnie left and went back to Tennessee. I never returned to what they called home. I meant that I wasn't going back. I could breathe and that was the feeling I wasn't willing to give up. I no longer had to worry about the rapes and neither the beatings.

I was free, although I was considered a runaway. What many wouldn't find out til later; I was pregnant; but I was grown. I was not the child that the beast lied that I was, even to those in the family. That's what I was trying to tell Lonnie this entire time. The lies that had been concealed for all these years; they would soon be exposed.

She, the beast would even tell my children later in life that I was only thirteen when I became pregnant with my child. That was a lie! What she neglected to tell my children; the one that she chose to tell that lie to, is that my pregnancy came from the rape of her brother or daddy. She neglected to tell my son that I was raped, and she beat me.

She failed to tell my son that she took me to the doctor; doctor Frank James and he gave me a little white pill that killed the baby that I carried, that killed the evidence inside of me to save her daddy and brother. My son believed what the beast told him as with the other lies she would poison him with. I was an adult now, things were different.

There was nothing that the beast could do, although she thought it was. She had no more control. I left, ran away until I became further along in my pregnancy. I didn't know what I would do, even how I would eat, but I would either survive or die trying. I dropped out of school in the tenth grade and lived on the streets.

I slept in convenient stores that were open all night long and walked the streets during the day. I meant that I would not get caught at this point. At night sometimes when I wouldn't go to the store, I would go to my favorite spot; the cemetery. When I didn't go to the cemetery, I would go over to a friends house and lay low.

I later met some friends that took me home with them. I didn't know that I was pregnant with twins. I would become sick from cigarette smoke. I moved to the country with my friends until I begin to get closer to my due date. One day, I was steady getting sick, and the elderly couple that I lived with in the country found out that I was pregnant.

They were so very overprotective of me. I love them because they went out their way, as did one of their daughters. I would have to go, one of their sons, tried to rape me. He didn't because I threw up on him. I was big enough for any and everyone to know that I had a baby on the way. Although I missed school; school was over for me.

For weeks, I enjoyed the country life. I would wake up to roosters crowing and watching empty fields over a beautiful sunrise blue sky. I would see the drops of dew on the tips of grass. There were no pavements, only the rocks that was hard on the tender bare feet, if walked naked on. Dust field the air as tractors mended the acres of field land.

I loved the country filled air. I loved everything about it; most of all, when I was in the country; this city girl felt closer to Christ. In the city, you could never enjoy the peace and love of the acres of land and the dust filled rocky roads, or watching the morning dew drops on the tips of rice growing in the fields ahead.

You could enjoy the beautiful lit skies at five o'clock in the morning as the sun beautifies the land or watching the sunset in the evening time over a fresh glass of lemonade. Yes, the country life was so peaceful and offered the serenity that the city life would never embrace you with. I have lots of dreams, but none like this.

I want a ranch house with five bedrooms and three baths and a guest house. I want a ranch house with horses, a husband and a playroom for the children and for their children to come. I want twenty-acres of land with a pond and stream of trees and greenery. Yes, I want it all. a deck and a pool, and a balcony, a bistro and my room designed only for me.

I was obsessed with the country; however, I was about to return to the pollution of smoking pipes attached to motorized cars, and jukejoints sitting on the corners of streets where the old hands are playing cards and shooting dice while listening to the blues on the created style jukeboxes. I was about to return to the hell filled streets.

I was about to return to the city where the people lacked the care and concern of Gods creation. A place where either the people chose not religion, chose religion and staying in church all day long, preventing people to fellowship with others, and others that were called street folks. Fancy clothes, High-heeled shoes, and dripped in gold, filled with sin.

While, I, Ava, impregnated with an angel growing inside of me, facing the toils of the beast where I had left in order to breathe a new life without the flames that burned my flesh for so many years; controlling my mere existence and stealing the very life out of my body; my lungs. It sicken me just to touch my soles to the tar that formed the streets.

Here, back in the city streets, I am trying to survive; to stay alive and to keep my growing baby inside of me alive. I knew that I had to face the past. I, Ava, The Runaway, was back. I was staying on the main streets on the Eastside of town. It wouldn't be long until the beast got wind that I am here. I was no longer afraid for me; however for my baby.

She was the queen of having babies aborted in order to hide the evil skeletons in her closet. Although I was an adult; the beast had stolen my identity from me. I was no longer the

Echols/Ford baby girl. I was no longer born in 1967; but 1969, and I was no longer born in Los Angeles, California, but in Little Rock, Arkansas, and my mom was no longer mom.

How would I prove that I was no longer a minor child? They sent one of the few people that I respected and adored in order to talk me into coming over to their house; my uncle. Why? They knew that if I saw either of them, it would be a cold day in hell before I would come to them. The beast words echoed in my head; your going to a reformatory home.

I didn't want the beast and no one else taking my baby. If I lost my baby, I would have no reason to live; because my life would be meaningless. Now, regardless of what the beast would tell those in front of me, around me, and even my children as years passed; I would turn nineteen that year I gave birth to my baby; not fifteen, and surely not thirteen.

I was about to turn nineteen; but her lies have captivated others for so long that everyone believed her. I don't even think pops knew my real age. I was ready to get this shit over with. Although I didn't know what was ahead of me, my stomach turned like a sicken virus that plagued the land. Each step I took seem to be long and hard.

My legs felt like a ton of boulders weighing me down. It was almost like I had been given a death sentence and was being forced to walk that last mile before the death chamber. I finally made it to the door, as everyone stood around waiting for me to walk in. I entered into the door as my uncle turned to go back onto the porch.

I saw a glow of happiness in Sunshine's eyes, I seen Pops leaned against the wall, as the beast raging red flamed eyes say's hi. She begins to talk to me, I didn't want to hear anything she said. She finally asked me if I was going to stay; No, was my reply. As I was getting ready to leave again, Pops grabbed me around my neck so I couldn't leave.

The beast told someone to call the police as he held me. I listened while she told the police dispatcher that I, her runaway was refusing to stay and she wanted me placed into a reformatory home. She neglected to tell them that I was carrying a child at the time. Because the beast knew that the police was coming, she didn't touch me.

She had Pops to subdue me in a choke hold. It was hurting. The police arrived, and she went outside to speak to them. As she spoke to them, another one entered into the house. He asked me if I was going to stay; No, I'm not staying here, I replied. I'll take my chances somewhere else! The beast face dropped as she watched me walk out the door.

The police placed me in the back of their cruiser and closed the door. As we rode, the officer begin to talk to me, as tears flowed like a roaring stream and memories embraced my mind; to me, I was finally free and I would show somehow that she was a liar. We made it to the courthouse and I was taken to an office and asked to wait.

Mrs Tommie Holmes came out greeted me. I didn't know my fate at the time; however, I knew that whatever happened, to me I was better off. I didn't know that she would be my ticket to freedom. I entered into her office and had a seat. She asked me, "What is so bad that I would ruin my life and give up such a wonderful place?"

I begin to tell her about my wonderful life. The life that you see as wonderful is a big dark hell that I have been locked in for years. I have been raped and I have been beaten. I have reported the abuse to those that you guys pay to protect us; however, they chose not too. What is better than this place?

The streets; because I have lived in hell since they have taken me from my biological mom. Mrs Holmes were trying to figure out what was next. She begin to type into her computer, she begin too, what seem to me; investigate. She asked me if I was hungry or wanted something to drink. The officer had informed Mrs. Holmes that I was being subdued.

I was being subdued in a choke hold and that's where the bruising or redness around my neck came from. As I sit in her office, she was in and out the door. She finally came and had a seat, her phone buzzed in; it was the beast. I couldn't hear what the beast was saying, however, from the sounds of it, she wanted me gone since I hadn't given in.

Mrs Holmes begin to question the beast about the discussions that had taken place in her office. The beast was outraged. Mrs Holmes informed me that I didn't have to go back. She asked me if I wanted to press charges on Pops for choking me; I told her No. I also informed her afterwards that I was pregnant and I was concerned about my unborn baby.

She told me that no one could make me give my baby up; as well that according to my records, that I was an adult. No one could make me do anything against my will. She also let me know that if anyone put their hands on me, especially being pregnant, that they would be prosecuted to the full extent of the law. I was free to go where I chose.

She even had an officer to drop me off at the place where I was staying at the time. I did call up there, I was trying to see if I could get my clothes; however, the beast was uncooperative. That was fine by me. I would work something out. Although I was pregnant, I only wore a size five. I wasn't very big at all. I was free. At least that is what I thought.

I no longer had to hide or run from the police. I no longer had to go to school or worry about, anyone or anything. I no longer had to worry about the abuse or misuse; and neither did I have to worry about the rapist. But I did. What would happened to my little cousin and my sister. I knew the beast wouldn't allow her close to me.

As long as I was doing wrong, and running from the police; I had help. But it seems as though when I elected to do right and stop running and hiding and everything was legal, no one wanted to help me. They were talking about me behind my back. Most became the very exact thing that I had been trying to get away from all my life.

One day, the lady that had taken my life, my identity, and brought darkness into my world; the woman I was forced to call mom and as I refer to as the beast of darkness in my life decided she would call me. I didn't want to talk with her; however, my associates convinced me to give her a chance,. I decided to listen to what she had to say.

However, as hard as I had tried, I couldn't believe a word she was saying. The break of silence down through the years never freed me. I was so angry that the only joy I ever felt, was knowing that I would one day be able to have a child to hold, to love, to care for, and that would hopefully love me back. Weeks had passed on by and I was getting larger.

I had only been to a clinic to make sure that the baby was okay and to get my prenatal vitamins. Apparently word got back to mother that I had lost an extreme amount of weight. Mother was my heart and she knew it. She called me, and I believe no one knew it. Anyone that knew me, knew that if anyone could get me to do anything, it would be her.

Mother invited me over for Sunday dinner. I explained to her, that I don't think that would be a good idea. She wasn't going to take No for an answer. She let me know that, she would drive and get me. Everyone knew, You didn't want her driving you anywhere. Everyone knew mother didn't know how to drive; she never learned in her earlier years.

I agreed to attend Sunday dinner, although I really didn't wont too because I knew that evil would be in the atmosphere. I couldn't let Sunshine down and I knew she was genuine. Sunday arrived and I kept my word. Like a stranger, I rung the doorbell and waited for someone to come to the door. Sis came to the door and mother was waiting for me.

I didn't know what to expect; my concern was only for the safety of my baby. Sunshine was the brightest ray of glory in the house. Darkness rested silently all around me. Not a mumbling word was spoken, other than hey. My sister smiled as she creep back to her room. Sunshine smiled as she was glad I came.

She say's, "I didn't think you were going to come." My sister was twelve at the time and living her life. I smelled familiar smells coming from the kitchen embracing my nostrils. Sunshine, say's, "I know your hungry, I prepared this meal especially for you, as she smiled at me. She called me to the kitchen; darkness ask me how had I been? Fine, I replied!

Sunshine beckon for me to come to the stove where she had all my favorite dishes that I had been craving for this entire pregnancy. Mustard and Turnip green leaves with hog jowl, ham hocks, and onions, Chitterlings, homemade cornbread dressing, peach cobbler, and blackberry cobbler. I was almost scared to eat; then I wondered well you know.

I wondered if I was about to be killed. I trusted Sunshine; however, there were a couple of dark silhouette shadows in the midst that I didn't trust and they were sitting right in front of me. Everyone wanted to talk; however, I, as usual, I would have loved to sit in silence. No one ever wanted to have anything to do with me, so I was accustom to that.

One would ask me how the baby was doing, the other would ask, what am I going to do about the baby? I'm going to keep it, what do I suppose to do; abort it, like; you know what, never mind. Sunshine, I think I am going to go; No your not, she replied. I fixed dinner for you and your going to eat. Ava, come home. You know you don't belong where you are.

You will have your own room, and won't have to worry about what your going to eat or anyone putting you out. You don't need to be around those folks and don't need to have your baby from house to house. Sunshine, I have endured enough hatred to last a life time. I don't want my baby around it, and I don't want to be around it.

I feel it and I know, that I have not ever been wanted here, so, why now, should I believe that things would be different. I don't want anyone saying they had to take care of me or mine. Sunshine looked at me and reassured me that she wanted me there. She told me that she would give me the bottom room if I wanted it, no one goes down there.

She was serious and she didn't want me to leave. I told her that I would pray about it and see; however, I wasn't a child and I wasn't going to be treated like one. I enjoyed the day over there, chilling and talking. Not to mention, the meal was fabulous as usual. I felt as though nothing as far as the behavior would change other than the physical abuse.

I would no longer have to worry about the rapes either, I didn't know what to do or what to think. One thing that I truly would do, is I would do what was best for my unborn child. As I ponder in deep thoughts, I knew that I was no longer a child and hadn't been a child even when I was tender in age, because I was forced to grow up fast.

Days and nights would pass me by as I enjoy this beautiful feeling of being able to carry a seed that would grow into a beautiful little boy or girl in a few months. I often wondered what life would bring to me now. I was broken, but forced to move on with my life. I was pieces of a jigsaw puzzle, I didn't know how to fix this brokenness.

CHAPTER EIGHT

As I sit today and think over my childhood and teenage life, I realize that I was so broken and destroyed. I realized that if my life didn't change, if I couldn't heal, then I would be everything that the beast said that I would be. I realized that at some point in our lives we must find a way to forgive those that hurt us.

Regardless of the pain that we have endured in life, we must be able to forgive those that hurt and spitefully misuses us. There are many reasons for me to hate, be bitter, angry, and even vengeful; if I was like others that had no heart.

There are reasons for me to allow darkness to consume my soul and become like the very exact ones that stoned me.

Love is a powerful emotion that everyone in life desire. Everyone is not loved by the very exact ones that they desire to be loved by. We as humans feel as though every man, woman, boy, and girl have a choice in life, and if we fail, it is our own fault. People that think in this manner are selfish, ungodly, and blind.

For many years I worked to become more than what I was told that I would be. I wanted to be a professional, with a successful career. I didn't want to live on welfare, struggle, and have to depend on others to find my way. Sometimes, we allow our blindness to hinder us from reaching the top by protecting and looking out for others.

Those very exact ones that we long for, their love, are the very exact ones that hindered my progress in life. It wasn't my choice to be in Jonesboro, Arkansas. I hated this place. However, even as a young adult, I allowed the very darkness that pulled me down to keep me down. I never thought that I could make it if I went out on my own.

The moment I chose to *Break the Silence*, after years of torture, torment, and darkness; That was the day that I begin to truly heal. It wasn't easy; however, I chose to realize why I couldn't excel in life. With all the pain and hurt, with all the trauma and loneliness, I deserved better. One thing that I learned years ago, is that no one cared.

You see, as an adult, I watched a cycle continue and

another generation become me. I couldn't have that on my conscious, as well, I wanted more for my babies. Breaking the silence, meant that the truth would unveil and those hidden secrets would be exposed that had been packed in cement filled locked cases for years.

Who am I to bring out the truth on these ratchet upstanding, hidden closet people; I am the wounded. You see, I didn't know how to not be who I was formed to be. I didn't know how not to respond or react when I was getting lied on, stepped on, and dogged out. I didn't know how not to protect mine when someone hurt them.

And I believe in my heart, my mom would have protected me by all cause if she could have. People are swift to judge others without evaluating the circumstances. They are swift to downgrade them, knowing that they wouldn't have survived half the trauma that others have endured. I have seen men and women kill themselves for lesser.

The kidnapping that took place in my earlier years, placed me in not only a detachment shock, but it was a cultural shock as well. Stripping me from my mom was the worse thing that could happen to me. Although, I had to learn how to adapt to my new environment and surroundings, I never got over the loss of my mom.

There was a love that already had formed, an unspeakable bond between a mother and her child. Not only was a bond removed, but an entire identity had been stricken away from me. I remember being thrown in the back of the back seat of this long car and a man was holding me. I was crying and screaming as they were hurting me.

Unlike other people that became a part of this family, I wasn't a baby. I was old enough to remember this horrific day. I remembered my mothers embrace and her love was stolen from me. Imagine if this had of been you. You carry your baby for forty weeks; one day, someone just snatch your child from you, without a trace; wouldn't you be lost?

Could you phantom the thought of losing one of your babies? Could you imagine someone taking your baby, changing their name, city and state, he or she was born, and the year they were born to make sure no one would locate them? Can you imagine, your baby being removed not only from your home and custody, but from your reach?

That's what happened to Ava. Ava knew that she did not belong in this household. She loved her mother so dearly that she sat day after day longing for her to come and take her home. Ava wasn't a bad child and neither did she do anyone wrong. Ava wanted what was rightfully hers to begin with and that was her mother.

You see, I angered the lady that forced me to call her mom, because I didn't know how to let my real mom go. I would sit and cry, wondering why did my mom not want me anymore. I realized that it wasn't my mom; if it was my biological mom, I wouldn't hold her this tightly in my heart as I have done. She never hurt me.

`This lady, the more she abused me the more I longed

for my mom. She would slap me in the face with this black-wide tooth comb. She would pull my hair and often let me know how much she hated the color of my hair. I thought acting out in school would make them send me back to my mom. They didn't understand that I didn't want them.

It was nothing personal, except this other woman hating my very appearance. She hated my hair so badly that she died it jet black and then through a perm in it, because it wouldn't stop curling and waving up. She wanted straight, black white folk hair on my head. I didn't understand why; what was wrong with my hair or my skin.

She didn't succeed on dying my hair. She left it in there quite some time; however, it would never take. My hair would only become brighter and the brown would shine like a ray of sun beaming off of my hair. Although I am a darker Caramel skin tone complexion now, back then I was a bright beautiful skin complexion. That wasn't good either.

That woman hated everything about me. When she hurt me or allowed me to be hurt, she would go back a few days later and try to talk to me or try to make it right by giving me money. My only safe haven was embracing the corners of a room, grabbing pencil or pen and paper and isolating my feelings on paper.

Suffering through blackouts, hiding within myself was the only way to survive. I was angry more than anyone could imagine around me. My violence started in elementary school, not junior high or high school. I remember the shortest teacher I would ever have, taking me in her room closet and paddling me for something I had done.

I think I might have hit a kid in the face on the playground. Mildred Kenner was her name. She was just a bit taller than I was. And then there was Mrs McBride, she was the first and only black teacher I would have. I think I might have had a substitute named Mrs Harris for awhile. Mrs McBride was a beautiful sophisticated teacher.

The bad thing about having Mrs McBride is that she knew these people I was now living with. I would often get beaten because I wasn't who she thought I should be; however, she had no clue, I wasn't who I knew I should be. I was being conformed into what someone else wanted me to be. I couldn't be who I was born to be.

The abuse became worse as I become older. I was often called retarded and eventually placed into a class for special children. I would stay in and out of the principal office as I became older even in elementary school. I attended East school from grades first to fifth and then moved on to Junior High School.

I wasn't allowed to have friends outside of school and lived as though I was in prison guarded by dogs and a barbed-wired fence. Playing, if I chose to do so, would be with only the children that lived in the Foster Care or were in this family. Needless to say, there were no girls at that time my age. There was only one girl that was older.

`Many years later, I would come to find out that this

older girl was my biological sister. There was only that one photo of me that I would only see if Sunshine was going through her photo album. That photo was me eating a piece of watermelon standing on the porch in my pink-pleated dress, black shoes, and puff balls.

`This white dirty house, with a small porch that seem to sit in the middle of nowhere, with no one but me and whomever was taken the picture. I seem to have lost an array of weight somewhere down the line, because I seen another frail and fragile picture of me. I looked at that photo, thinking to myself; maybe, this is why my mom is gone.

I was in girls scouts and even the 4H club; it wasn't enough to take my mind off of my mom. I don't know how old I was when I made it here, but they should have known that I was old enough to remember her an I would long for her love, because they didn't have love for me. The day that I would Break the Silence; would be the change for me.

The State of Arkansas and the City of Jonesboro owes me my life back; say's Ava! I never wanted to be here and neither did my mom choose for me to be here. When I asked Ava why do she feel as though the City and State owe her anything; her answers left me in tears. I was born to my mom and my dad, which was not a resident of this State.

They crossed the state line and brought me to the City of Jonesboro and the State of Arkansas. It wasn't my mom or dad that did this to me and neither was it Child Protective Services, removing me from my mom because she neglected me. Everyone else is obsolete and committed a crime. This includes those that took me in, grandparents, and the city.

The State became a part of this crime when they approved a fictitious birth certificate that they couldn't even get together. I couldn't even get a birth certificate until 2001 or 2002. When I got my driver's license, I didn't show a birth certificate and neither a high school transcript as I was given some lame ass excuse.

No one knows how it feels to have the woman that you are forced to call mama, to stand in the doorway of her bedroom and tell you to your face that you knew that she would be a BITCH JUST LIKE HER MOM! She was telling me that. She told me that my mom was a loose-legged hoe and I was going to be just like her.

They told my brother that he was going to be trouble. I wanted to tell them, that she, the beast was his trouble. I feel as though the State of Arkansas and the City of Jonesboro not only owe me for the kidnapping, but they owe me for the abuse that they allowed to go on, and the rapes. They knew about it all, yet they turned their heads.

This Natural State allowed my little fragile body to be abused, ripped, worn, and shredded by grown men and closed a blinded eye and a deaf ear. They ignored my cries for help for many of years including my childhood years. They allowed me to be enslaved and held captive. Even with the evidence presented to them, they yet failed me; us.

They allowed me to endure this physical, emotional

and mental anguish with pride. Just because I did not crash and lose my mind like the Menendez boys and go on a killing spree, they owe me a lifetime of mental health counseling to try and piece my life back together again. Rape have no statue of limitation, yet the rapist is free.

He has continued to rape and molest girls and the City of Jonesboro have allowed him to get away with it. His sister not only beat the hell out of me with an orange outdoor extension cord; because that's all she could find at the time to beat me with; but she eventually burned the house down year's later taking everything with it.

Believe it or not, I yet, had those very exact clothes that he raped me in hidden away; for what, because he was my first rapist. The State not only owe me retribution, but they owe Johnny, Terra, and Sherry. Those babies suffered their stay at the Washington Street Alcatraz, as did Jerry suffer at the hands of the rapist.

While some of us held on with the mustard seed of faith that we knew, others, I don't believe was so fortunate. I suffer from blackouts, which leave many gaps and bridges throughout my years. To conceal the evidence of rape by aborting the baby is a crime and mental cruelty. This is what happened to me; this is what happened to us.

The lies that were told, the deceit, and all the illegal acts the City of Jonesboro, that black lying, crooked ass pastor that everyone so loved, the attorney, all played their parts in the corruption that took place in my childhood. I have just wanted a chance in life to regain what was stolen from me as a child and a teenager.

I never chose to hurt anyone! I don't like pain, evil, and deception or manipulation. I never wanted anyone in trouble; just to pay for the injuries that they inflicted on me and others like me. I know that a lot have been taken away from me and time has swiftly passed me by. I have become comfortable in being alone and without a family.

I believe that I deserve the right to be reunited with my mom and I believe that I have the right to know all thirteen of my brothers and sisters and if they choose not to see me, that is fine also. It does not stop me from loving the sister and brother that I was reared up in the household with and neither will it stop me from loving my biological family.

To steal and deprive a child of their mothers love, is pure evil when she did not deserve it. I remember when the beast worked and set a plot to rob me of my daughter. I fought that evilness to the very end. I refused to give up, I stood up and I fought; however, my mom didn't stand a chance. The trail of deception died with them.

You see, today, the devil in hell wants to make me think that each and every person that did me wrong has gotten away with it because they have perished this life. All those dark closet secrets; well, whose going to believe them? Satan would like to make me think that there will never be healing and retribution for the darkness.

But one thing that the devil in hell knows oh to well;

we must all pay for our sins, in this life and the after life. The abuse is duly noted. The lies and torture that the beast had everyone believing and the torture that she administered must be answered to by Christ the Savior. The rapes and lies, will all come out, it will be exposed one day.

No one cared if I healed, became a success, or even excelled in life. They did care about their future and that is all they focused on. They never cared about me or my children unless they needed to use them to continue to climb the ladder, freeing up time to live a lavish life, showing their friends a good time, and so forth.

These people didn't want to have anything to do with you unless you benefit them. Today, I have gotten so use to being by myself that the feeling of loneliness is not the same. I would love to have a good time and live life a little. I haven't tried or even desired to be caved up like a bear in hibernation, but I refuse to be the new carpet rolled out.

Neither do I choose to be an old refurbished carpet handed down to a homeless family as if I didn't deserve to be treated equally, more so than those that spend their lives refusing to admit their wrongs and judgmental blindness. I never treated anyone wrong, and it is not wrong for me to seek retribution for the darkness that covered me for so long.

It's not easy trying to let go of the past when you were never allowed to live from the beginning. Today, you look at me and label names for me in the professional world in order to conceal the truth of those demons that you glorify with sunshine trying to hold me captive in darkness. It's very easy to love those who have shown you love.

And sometimes those that have shown you love from day one, you cannot show love to because their ability to succeed in life was limited because of the sacrificial love offered to others. Does that make them less than a human than you are? My heart, now, I can see was far more genuine than those placed in my path.

I could never stop myself from loving those that didn't have the ability to love me and even my enemies. Do I hate anyone; of course not! How did I manager to keep my sanity through all of my trials and throughout my journey? This life has nothing to do with me. You see, I cried for so many years; said Ava! And some would say; oh she's crazy!

The only love that I had was the seeds that were planted within me and that I nurtured into full bloom. I never stopped nurturing and neither did I leave my seeds to water themselves. I fell sometimes, maybe a lot of times, however, the only love that I ever knew or could even remember, was that love I once felt from my mom.

The only love that I had in my life now, was the love of my seeds. The love of watching them being birthed into this cruel world, the love of protecting them and keeping them from evil, although evil was all around them. The only love that I held onto; is the love that I felt for each one of those blossoms that I once held in my arms so tightly.

I didn't know if what I felt for my babies were love or

an obsession. Was I mentally deranged? Was love the vile kidnapping and illegal acts that I endured? Was love the defamation of character that I sustained because of the undying love for my mom that couldn't be beaten, torn, or buried six-feet under like a dead corpse.

What was love? All I knew is that the only rays of sun that filled my heart was the seeds that Christ blessed me with. This other life, the beatings, torture, the rapes; all were darkness that filled my life as a child and teenager, I was confused and mortified with unbelief. I couldn't get passed this pain. I cried for help, yet no one would listen to me.

What hurt me more than every beating, every lie that was told on me, and every stone from people that I endured; other than when they stole me from my mom, is the first rape that I endured. I didn't ask for it, I wasn't a tease, and I wasn't a fass little girl that went after old ass married men. I was placed in this house only to be a tool for them.

This grown ass married man; the beast brother, with a whole family of his own, ripped my gold mine apart. He thought it was funny, he thought it was cute. He didn't care what or how I felt. It wasn't funny to me now and neither back then. Feeling his big black slimy dick going into my tender virgin area; turning my vagina into just a pussy.

He has no remorse at all about what he done to me and neither to many before me. Then if that wasn't enough; he poked his chest out in honor, and every time he is near, I get this sicken feeling in my stomach. I was tortured for so many years, having to see and be around him as if nothing had ever happened. Then she beat me, to shut me up.

The woman that I called a beast, the woman that I was given to, that I was forced to call mama; as if her brother tearing my pussy apart wasn't bad enough, she beat me with an orange outdoor extension cord, she called me all kinds of bitches and sluts and liars because I had the dirt off of his uniform in the back of my hair.

I wasn't a machine, I had feelings once a point of time in my life, but that day, my feelings became like the debris in a disintegrator; they evaporated into thin air. For years I have adopted darkness and all I wanted was love, a real unconditional family of my own, and equality. I never wanted to hurt anyone, but I wanted my mom and siblings.

Yet, I know that the damage have already been done. I got over my pain, only in 2009. I was forty-two years of age. I had spent my adult life trying to piece this puzzle back together so that I would be free. I spent the majority of my life worried about others and neglecting myself. I removed myself from church at the time.

I found that the largest hypocrites were in church, rather than out on the streets. The pastor of First Baptist Church on Kitchen Street is the culprit that allowed this family to continue the lies and deception. He even had the files in 2001 when I was conducting an investigation on the family and on my family. I was trying to find me!

Mommy dearest became in raged in anger she was

furious. The hypocrite they called a pastor at that church held my life line in his hands; Lewellan was what they called him, one of those old Baptist preachers that wouldn't talk to women, only to the male people in the household. Little did he know that the leader of this family was a she.

Although, he offered the file to Mommy dearest husband, he had no say so in anything around here. I listened to him on the phone as he reassured the beast and family that he would not relinquish the file to me, but let them know that my biological mom was still alive and she had fourteen children and she yet lived in California.

I wasn't trying to destroy a family, I was trying to complete my family. I was trying to bury my horrific past and start a new chapter in my life if that was even possible. What people are failing to realize in this twisted tangle web, is that, had the truth been told before, it would have destroyed many lives, more than mine.

I am no longer concerned about who care to understand my pain, my agony, or my grief. I furthermore, do not care about the opinions and comments of people that never cared for me in the beginning. If you hate me now, it's not because I have lied or attempted to degrade anyone, I've only spoken the truth as I will always do.

I am here today, only because of "Yeshua" the Christ. It was my spiritual connection that allowed me to continue to love people, especially those that condemned me, stoned me, and left me to rot and die by myself. It was my spiritual connection that allowed me to forgive all of those people that have hurt me along the way.

It is my spiritual connection that have allowed me to know who I am and that I have a Divine Purpose in this life. Along this journey, I wouldn't know the meaning of how to trust or have my faith in someone. Along my journey, I have taught many people the true genuine meaning of love and forgiveness. And it is the Savior that showed me how.

You see, there are many of you out here that believe that either there is no God the Father, Jesus the Son, or the Holy Ghost. Some of you are your own god. Or maybe you believe in some other Religion including Muhammad. You are a textbook guru that knows it all. You have the answers to every obstacles that I have endured.

And there are others that choose to remain blind because that is their comfort zone. You will not allow the truth to embrace you. It is easier to continue to dislike and pull down the victim oppose to facing the truth. You can't face the truth, that the very ones you loved, could be so evil. People choose to help, love, and support the unknown.

It is easier to help people that you do not know and that you meet along the way, than those that have disclosed the secrets of darkness that a victim have exposed. It is easier to conceal the truth by not facing it and running away from it. It is easier to stone those that have been lied on and treated like trash because you have accepted the darkness.

The darkness that covered you that voice in your head

and in your heart that you knew was wrong, the lies you knew was wrong, the maltreatment that you knew were wrong, but you accepted it only because you didn't have to face those challenges and neither did your seeds. Your life of darkness allows you to maintain control.

Could you really handle the true reality of those that you once looked up too or that you yet played as your heroes? Only to find out the evil, hatred, and maltreatment that they once administered to those that you said you loved? So many have believed and embraced the darkness that it hurts them to have a relationship with the victims.

I am not bitter, and I am not holding on to the darkness. It wasn't easy moving on and burying the hurt and pain that I have endured along my journey. It was not easy sitting back watching yourself suffer although everything in you wants to throw in the towel. You have figured out many reasons to die. People show more love dead than alive.

Don't look like your in shock; yes, people that say they love you; will show you more love stretched in a casket in front of a pulpit than they will alive. Well, I believe that your bartered love, you can save. I give my flowers to those that I love while they can enjoy them. Many people speak of holiness and righteousness, for what purpose?

I speak of love because the love of Christ is what pulled me through my suicidal days. I wanted to die, and have attempted it more than once, but I always botched it up. I didn't deserve the treatment that I was getting; no one does! I was always blunt and bold with whatever the situation would be. I didn't hide what I did or how I felt.

I have always been an open book. If you didn't like me that was your loss. I love people where they are and not what others want them to be. I can love you from a distance or up close. I really didn't know me, I thought that I was the problem because as a child, this is what I was made to believe. I had no self-esteem and I suffered from an eating disorder.

It was nothing to see my rage and anger through the violence that I embraced. Not on the innocent but on those that stepped to me in a not so nice manner. I couldn't find my rightful place in this life. I was like no one around me, I was the outcast, the brawny paper towel that you wiped up your spills with. I was in this world alone, is how I felt.

How could you understand, you couldn't possibly know what I was dealing with. But Christ did, for it was God that created me; who could know me better? I was taught to never question God, Don't ask him questions, just do it! Whatever happens deal with it; it's something that you are not doing, your bad and rotten, your cursed.

You need to pray and not ask questions. That is the worse thing that an adult could say to a wounded child, teenager, or even another adult. And the sad and sick part of it all; it is you holy rollers that are killing the hurt spiritually to the point of no return. However, I found out, through my journey that, everyone cannot give answers to your problems.

How can man answer questions and provide solutions

for healing when they are the very exact ones that inflicted the pain and hurt? They are the very exact ones that ripped your life apart to begin with and they are the very exact ones that had no meaning of love. I knew that, "He" knew my name before my parents named me from birth.

Christ knew my struggles and my strains, he knew the obstacles that I would endure and He had a divine purpose for me. I had no other alternative but to seek Christ for my answers. If you have not endured heartache and pain, struggles and strains, if you hadn't endured the wrath of evil, then you have no clue to what I am talking about.

Unlike others that had been around me daily and knew that I was not the kind of girl that I was being portrayed to be; Christ sits high and looks low. God, saw all that I was enduring. Christ would allow His Angels to visit me. That's how I knew that Christ is for real, regardless of what things may look like, someone was watching over me.

I didn't trust Him at the time. I'm not ashamed to say it, I didn't. I didn't want to hear about church when I became older and neither did I want to hear about God. I was even visited by an Angel when I was thirteen and I knew what I had seen, yet, didn't believe, because how could He be of so much love and allow me to be destroyed, if He loved me?

Now, I was angry with this God the Father and with His Son Jesus; Yeshua, the man that gave His life for me; yet he couldn't save me from the beast and her mates? No, I would take my chance on the streets. Now, don't get me wrong, I hated Satan and his workers with a passion. I wanted to kill him and his advocates, but there were so many.

I remained in my own little world, not believing in anything and anybody. Why should I, and how could I? I would never be able on my own to eradicate the evil that could only grow in time in this society. I look around me and I see the good selling out, and the evil becoming stronger.

As a strange child and even a stranger teenager, Satan goal was to have me destroyed, to bring me over permanently to his side. I did what I wanted to do, whenever I wanted to do it. No one cared and no one would stop me, just as no one stopped the beatings and no one stopped the rapes. However, I knew that I was lost in darkness.

Although my anger was not falsified, I didn't' hurt anyone, or even think about hurting someone that did not hurt me or others. I enjoyed having fun and smiling. I loved being around people of like mind. The nightmares were horrific and the pain was great, yet I had to keep pushing. Something inside of me wouldn't allow me to give up.

No one knew of the agony that I would endure for years. I knew that I would never be who they wanted me to be regardless of how hard I tried. I enjoyed making people smile and feel good, even if no one cared about how I feel or showing me the same feeling. I would show others the love that I desired.

I never thought twice about it, regardless of how I felt, I was going to show others the love that I wanted others to show me. It seems like the more I helped and showed others love, the better I felt. I know that Christ is the reason I survived. This mystical, rare heart that I possessed could never be replaced. Maybe I could show the beast how to love.

Although fear embraced me, I had to move around daily. It was that rare heart within me that had a connection that was explainable, that was not connected to any portion of this world. I was different and I needed to know why? I needed to know me and what was it about me that was not like others. Who am I really?

CHAPTER NINE

am Ava, through all the brokenness and pain. I am a loving, kind, and bruised soul. I was born in Los Angeles, California on April 11th, 1967. I found out that my Mother Maiden Last name was Ford and my biological dad last name was Echols. My name is not my birth name and my social security number is not my social security number.

The day that man through me in the back of that long car, transporting me to this state, was the day that I lost my identity. I was beaten and conformed to adapt to life in the

State of Arkansas. I was raped and broken into pieces; sex is all I begin to know. What you have read is the life I grew up under. I don't know how to hate and remain bitter.

My life was never a fairy-tale, and I endured great pain and heartache. What you have read in *A Lonely Dove, You Stoned Me; But God Owns Me, and now in The Break of Silence,* is the life that I endured as a child and as a teenager. Sometimes, I have learned in this life, you must go through Long-Suffering in order to reach your divine destiny.

Everyone has an Eternal Purpose. So many people say that they are Christians, yet they are only Christians and have no clue with what being Christ Like or a Saint really means. They have no clue of what love means. Love is an action word that speaks volumes all by itself. Love is not hurt, pain and deception; neither manipulation and darkness.

I yet suffer from major "Blackouts" due to the horrific maltreatment that I endured. People heard me but no one ever listened to me. As you read throughout this book, you will see many skips and questions; Time periods that is missing from my life. I seek counseling in order to try to regain memories back on today. I will never give up.

It was my relationship with Yeshua the Christ that allowed me to overcome the darkness. It wasn't until later in life that I tasted freedom for the first time. The more I grew in Christ, the closer we became. I had to obtain a personal relationship with Yeshua, before the weight of my childhood was lifted up off of me.

Standing outdoors, while the children were bedded down, I had a little talk with Yeshua the Christ; I told Him all about my trouble, confessed all my sins, desires, and my faults. I humbled myself as I begin to work for the Kingdom. Many dignitaries walked over me. Many nights I laid in my bed, filled with tears and brokenness once again.

Although I was hurting and in pain, this pain was different. You see, the evening I stood outdoors and had that little talk with Yeshua, the Christ; it was not like anything I had ever seen or felt in my life. That summer evening, in the smothering heat, no wind was blowing, except at that one teary moment, a gust of wind released my shoulders.

You don't understand; "This was no ordinary wind!" The wind that grabbed my shoulders, removed mountains of boulders from my soul and then I excelled. I begin to smile as I continued to speak to Yeshua the Christ as I would spend the next few years continuing to heal. It was only because of the blood that He shed on the cross that I yet lived.

Many day's and nights I researched and analyzed my life. I didn't understand what was going on in my life. I didn't understand why all the bad things happened to me. It wasn't so much as how horrific the circumstances were, but it was the evilness behind the events. It was because the closet thing to Christ is a child. Yet, it was children that were hurt.

I asked Christ to forgive me for my sins, for the wrongs that I have done in my life. I told him that I would never be perfect, and that I make many mistakes regardless of how hard I try, but I asked him to fix me and all of my brokenness. I searched my soul, long and hard. I searched for years, trying to find out if I wronged others.

My heart is content, because all I have offered anyone is true love, regardless of how they have chosen to treat me. There are issues that I yet work through; however, I am the property of God. I was created by Him in order to change the meaning of the word of "Love" that so many people abuse today. I remain imperfect. But I am genuine and true.

It is your loss if you choose not to know me, or if your choice have been to misuse and abuse my love. It is further your choice if you choose to deceive, humiliate, and degrade me; because when you do, you are hurting Yeshua the Christ. I will never change for the people on this earth. I have a divine purpose and despite Satan working to destroy me; I made it.

To those that are hurt and wounded, have given up on life, please hold on; God is not threw with you yet. Regardless of what your pain may be in this life; you have a divine purpose. Know that God has something greater for you. How do I know? because I am here as a living testimony for you. With all the pain I endured; I have the victory!

Today, I am the proud mother of seven beautiful children. Although, I dropped out of school in the tenth-grade, I later went back to school, studied, and obtained my Arkansas High School Diploma and that was after giving birth to five children. After two failed marriages, and a life of struggles, I still wouldn't give up.

I obtained my Associates in Paralegal Studies and a Special Associates in Business Management. I worked in the community directing After School Programs for At-Risk Students. I worked as a Counselor through my Evangelistic Ministry while working to better the community. I later went on to pursue my Bachelor's in Sociology.

I didn't stop there, when my daughter and one of my sons had taken sick in my junior year at Arkansas State University; The University would not work with me and neither would the professors. I worked countless hours to obtain my degree. I was working towards a minor in Psychology and Human Sexuality.

I had to leave Arkansas State University in order for my child to receive medical treatments in Little Rock. The University held that against me, held my transcripts, so I could not transfer to another University; Yet, I was determined to achieve higher. Yes, I started all over again and this time, I majored in Psychology with a minor in Criminal Justice.

Today, I am a writer! The year I was set to graduate, just two months before graduation, my Financial Adviser came to my classroom; the last class that I was to take, which was Statistics, and informed me that I had ran out of Financial Aid and would have to fund the last 9 hours out of pocket. I was set to graduate, and now everything I worked for is over?

University of Phoenix couldn't explain where my Five-thousand dollars were, or the reason why I couldn't graduate with my colleagues. Now, I am ready to snap. I have a new baby, divorced, and I have two sick children and I'm all alone. I never stopped striving for what I wanted. I worked my butt off and met my obstacles head on as I continued my path.

My faith in Christ, and my dedication to God allowed me to rise above all attacks that I had to face. After my divorce, my children and I became homeless. No one knew it because, no one cared to check up on me and my babies. My baby had to have corrective eye surgery, and I worked day in and day out to survive and provide for my babies.

I would hear the bitter words from my ex-husband and I had no help and no support. I eventually begin to pay others for my children to have a roof over their heads. However, this is another book for another time. I refused to give up despite any obstacle that I faced in my life. I didn't allow the horrific memories of my childhood and teenage life to stop me .

I did not allow the cruel and evil people in this world to dictate and neither control my love and how I treated people regardless of who it was. The more I became more involved in church, paid my tithes and offering, and worked for the Lord to change my circumstances; seems like the more Satan attacked me and my family.

People still used me, walked over me and disgraced me. They still stoned me, disowned me, and talked about me and my babies, yet I held on. I never worked to impress others. I had people watching me when I didn't even know it, and yet could care less about my situation. I wasn't a bum or a lady of the streets; even if I was, everyone needs help.

I enjoyed feeding the homeless, yes, although me and my babies were homeless. Yes, I wanted to go on vacation for a change. I wanted to take my children on vacation and also buy them nice things or be able to pay for trips and give them allowances like other children their age; however, it never worked out that way,

I thank God for His Mercy and for His grace because He never let me down. I will never be who you want me to be, but I will always be who God wants me to be. I have realized that my reward can not be given by man; but my reward is given through Christ Jesus our Lord and Savior. I thank God for the gifts that He has already blessed me with.

I thank Him for all my blessings to come. I now know that I was special from my mom's conception. I will not stop believing in Christ, because of him, I can reach my eternal divine destination. This life is larger than what many people could ever imagine. It is He that kept me as a child and as a teenager. It is He; Yeshua the Christ, that kept me!

Your test and trials only makes you stronger if you are able to survive. The way that you survive is through Christ Jesus. You will never understand my strength, and my relationship with Christ if you haven't received Christ as your Personal Savior. You must truly believe and operate with a clean heart. It is easy for you to lie to ordinary people.

You can buy most people in this world, but you can't buy God; He doesn't have a price tag on Him, but if you seek Him; if you seek Yeshua, the Christ, you will taste what real freedom means. So, I may not be where you feel like I should be. I may not be who you want me to be, but I am who Christ created me to be.

Never allow your past to dictate your present and neither your future. Never allow anyone to control your pathway, through your hurt and pain. Never allow yourself to be handicapped by the evil that was placed in front of you to block your pathway to each color of your rainbow. Pray without ceasing and know that Yeshua, the Christ hears you.

THE AUTHOR

Hi, I am Imani and many children and teenagers are faced with child abuse and rapes on a daily basis. Many are ignored and tarred like the pavement that people drive over and doesn't think twice about the possibility of it collapsing. What is even more sad; so many people have no clue what loves mean; that by the time they figure it out, it is too late.

For many years, I actually thought that I was insane; however, I wasn't. I knew what true love was really about. I was able to figure out my divine purpose before it was to late; many will not have the chance to right his or her wrong, primarily, because of their pride. Pride, evilness, control, and power are all evil works that control the mindset of many people including the young.

My gift to others are the gift of love. I had no choice as a child; however, as an adult, I have had the choice to do what I know is right; although, the blinders of evil consumed me for so many years. Although the trauma that I endured as a child was wrong, horrific, and as evil as an adult could do to a child/children, and even to adults; I had to forgive each and everyone of them.

The moral to my life story as a child and as a teenager; is loving past your pain. Loving despite the obstacles that you may face. It is not for us to be vengeful and neither judge others. It is for us to pray and believe Gods word that He would make our enemies our footstool. Our enemies are those that hurt us, no matter how much we love them and do right by them.

Love past your pain and forgive those that hate you; Watch God stand on His Word!